PLENTY TOO MUCH
Making Your Biggest Difference

PLENTY
TOO
MUCH

Making Your Biggest Difference

DALE WALKER

XULON PRESS

Xulon Press
2301 Lucien Way #415
Maitland, FL 32751
407.339.4217
www.xulonpress.com

Printed in the United States of America.

ISBN-13: 978-1-6305-0544-8

About the Cover: Victoria Falls, Zambia, Africa

The Zambezi River is one of the greatest sources of life-giving water in the world. It flows over Victoria Falls, one of the largest falls in the world. The river winds through six countries where many people are suffering from the devastating effects of poverty. This scene is a reminder of our gracious God, who longs for His infinite supply to flow through us to those in need.

TABLE OF CONTENTS

FORWARD

I have found the title *Plenty Too Much* to be a powerful inspiration to believers, and because of the truths of this masterpiece, I scarcely put the book down before reading it in about 6 hours. Due to the simple and powerful veracity based on Jesus feeding the 5,000, it is a confirmation that the truths of the Word of God are never old, Hallelujah!!!

After walking and giving by faith for more than seven decades in the mission field of the world, I agree from the depth of my heart that the revelation God has given Pastor Dale Walker is a lifestyle of living and walking in the footsteps of Jesus, who came not to receive but to give and not to be served but to serve (Mk.10:45).

It is my prayer that multitudes of God's precious people will be inspired by this book and motivated to hasten the return of our Lord Jesus, by investing more and more of their time and talents in world harvest.

Jesus said: This gospel, must be preached in all the world before we are privileged to attend the Marriage Supper of the Lamb (Mk.13:10). Glorious day!!

Wayne Myers, author of *Living Beyond the Possible* and *Honor Your Call*

ENDORSEMENTS

Dale Walker is not only a faithful father, grandfather, husband, missionary, pastor and author, he is my big brother. For as long as I can remember he's always been one of those people that inspires and motivates people to be all that they can be through the power of God's spirit! This book is yet another great example of this. I believe the title and words in this book are a prophetic and incredibly timely word for many, including myself! I believe the way you perceive your life and resources will never be the same!

Tommy Walker,
worship leader, songwriter and author

During the process of co-editing *Plenty Too Much*, I faced hard decisions in my personal life. I was feeling led to attempt adopting my granddaughter, against many odds, and had serious doubts whether I had the financial, physical, emotional and spiritual means, or the favor of the court to actually carry it out. A few months into the process, my sister and I were suddenly responsible for the 24/7 in-home care of our 92-year old dad in hospice. I wondered if I was going to be able to do all of this, feeling like giving up. As I read and re-read the book, I was strengthened and encouraged that yes, I CAN step out and trust God to supply more than I need to do what He is calling me to do. And He is doing just that!

Rhonda Lehman

After witnessing the extraordinary, have you looked down on your ordinary? I have. This kind of thinking is challenged in *Plenty Too Much*. The book challenges me to see the ordinary, in God's hands, making our biggest difference. It inspires me to give Jesus every part of everyday, no matter how ordinary it may seem. Instead of looking down on the ordinary, I celebrate because He is overwhelmingly EXTRAORDINARY!

Vivian Brown

As I was editing this book, it occurred to me that this is all about the good news. As Pastor Dale writes, "A plenty too much mindset is one in which we look at, plan and act toward needs based on what is in God's pocket, not ours."

What a comfort, for our own pockets are not always brimming – or filled with wisdom that would benefit us and/or our loved ones. Even before I became a Christian, my most profound life transformations (meeting my wife, landing that dream job) were made possible when I simply got out of the way. Now that I understand why, I remind myself daily to turn my course over to Jesus and thank Him for all my blessings.

Marty Racine

INTRODUCTION

A ship had lost its bearings and was drifting at sea. The crew ran out of fresh water and assumed they were going to die. Thankfully, they saw another ship approaching. As it came alongside, the desperate crew cried out begging for water. What they didn't know was that they had drifted to a spot offshore where the fresh water of the Amazon River was flowing into the ocean. The captain of the rescuing ship shouted to the desperate men, "Let down your buckets." They quickly did and retrieved more fresh water than they could drink.

I believe this story illustrates the situation so many Christians are experiencing. There is a daily contradiction between the abundant life Jesus has provided, and what they are actually living. Oh, how awesome it is that God's 'Amazon River' of provision flows not only near, but in us by the Holy Spirit, if we can learn to "let down our buckets."

The Gospel teaches of the lavish richness of God's love and grace. God didn't merely say He loves us, He gave His only begotten Son for us. Jesus didn't just come to Earth; He became our Substitute. He took our grief, bore our sorrows and sickness, became poor for us in every way that we can be poor, so that through His poverty we can be rich, extravagantly provided for in all that *pertains to life and godliness*. (Isa. 53:4-6; 2 Cor. 8:9; 2 Pet. 1:3 NKJV)

"It is finished," was His powerful cry from the Cross. Everything that needed to be paid for was paid. There was not one part of our redemption, our full adoption and inheritance that wasn't provided. His gift of righteousness and the abundance of grace provide more than enough for us to reign in life through Christ Jesus (Rom. 5:17).

Why, then, do we often fall short of our full inheritance in Christ? In the pages to come, I will share from my journey principles from God's Word that have helped me experience more of God's fullness. You will see that it isn't about having more for us.

The point of understanding and applying the truths of receiving the sufficiency of God's grace is so that Jesus can 'have the fruit of His sufferings' (as the early Moravians used to say). Our good, good Father longs for those who are lost and have the least chance of knowing a life of hope, health, and security. God wants us to receive our full blessing so that all of the nations of the world might be blessed.

As I considered how to tie together the different pieces of the book's theme of living from an abundance mindset, I kept returning to the familiar story in the Gospel about

Jesus multiplying the loaves and fishes from a little boy's lunch that he willingly gave to Jesus. I believe that this story really exemplified the life of living in abundance that I want to convey. I hope that, in the story of our lives, we can move from playing the role of the consuming crowd to walking in the shoes of the extravagantly generous boy, who saw his small lunch become plenty too much.

I am so grateful for the writing team and my precious natural and church family who have lifted me up in completing this book. Thank you, Rhonda, Vivian, Marty, Anna and so many who have contributed.

Dale
2019

Chapter 1

A LIFE WITHOUT LACK

"And God is able to make all grace abound towards you, that you, always having all sufficiency in all things, may have an abundance for every good work" (2 Cor. 9:8 NKJV).

Jesus has been telling us some amazing things about the power of faith. I wonder what would happen if I took a step of faith. What if I wasn't afraid of not having enough for me? What if I gave all I have to Jesus? Would He somehow make a way for me to have my needs met? It's not much, just five loaves of bread and two small fish. But it's a start. It's the little I can do to help all of these hungry people. Besides, if I give it to Jesus, there's no telling what He could do with it.

I'm imagining what might have been going on inside the mind of a little boy who gave his lunch to Jesus. This famous story told in all four gospels is one that has deeply challenged my life. It is so amazing that a young child who probably had the least will always be known as the one who was used to provide for one of the biggest banquets in history.

1

More importantly, it seems Jesus memorialized this story to show us in a practical way what it means to trust and believe for God's abundance to flow miraculously on behalf of people in need.

Of course, I don't know what the boy was thinking. I do know I have asked similar questions. Perhaps you too have felt the tension between a "just me" and "I wonder what God could do through me" mindset. There has been a lot written about the difference between a scarcity mindset and an abundance mindset. I believe that it's worthy of another look, especially from a mission and compassion perspective. As we consider the billions without Christ and so many in extreme poverty, it makes great sense to consider how all of us as Christians could stretch our faith. If we would follow the example of a little boy and, in Jesus's name, take some bold actions, imagine what surprising ways God could use our little to accomplish much.

I serve an amazing church family who, along with partnering businesses, ministries and individuals has, over the past 20 years, attempted to dramatically shift from a scarcity mindset to an abundance mindset for the sake of the lost and impoverished. Heart for the World began as a mission organization and now includes a small group of churches. Our passion is to see what we can do to take God's extravagant heart to transform a desperate world. We've discovered how important it is to believe God for His unlimited resources to accomplish this otherwise impossible task.

I've always been stirred by Paul's challenge to financially strapped churches in ancient Macedonia that followed in the little boy's steps. He wrote these amazing words, *"And God is able to make all grace abound towards you, that you, always having all sufficiency in all things, may have an abundance for every good work"* (2 Cor. 9:8 NKJV).

I haven't always had this mindset. I still find it easier to slip back sometimes into a scarcity mindset. But God did something that stretched my world years ago. I was a busy pastor who had rarely considered the needs of overseas missions. We had just purchased a building and I was just trying to keep up with the demands of a growing congregation, when I got a call asking if I would like to have a pastor from the Philippines give a testimony in our Sunday evening service. I'm not even sure why I said "Yes." But as Pastor Levi told how scores of pastors were giving their lives to take the gospel to remote places, fasting for weeks because they didn't even have enough food to eat, my heart was broken.

I began an incredible journey that involved committing a six-week *tithe* of my calendar year to serve in the Philippines and eventually, other countries. In the most positive way I can describe, this adventure wrecked me from my small-world perspective.

On one of those trips, I had an unusual experience that confirmed to me that God indeed wanted to do through us (and all of His people) more than we could ever ask or think.

3

I was on an outreach with a church group in Cebu, Philippines. The church was ministering to people who lived as squatters in a graveyard. They would use the tombs as tables and beds. There were open graves kids could fall into.

Like usual, the kids surrounded us with giggles of joy and laughter. Oh, how they loved the games and especially the candy. I will never forget picking up a little 3-year-old girl dressed in rags. I blessed her and began to put her down. As I did, she threw her arms around my neck and just wouldn't let go. Several times I attempted to put her down, but she just kept clinging. I ended up leading worship and giving my message with the little girl's arms around my neck.

"What would you do if that was your little girl?" Later, as I reflected on this, I felt God speaking to my heart, "What would you do if that was your little girl?" I have four daughters and I took that question very personally.

I said, "I would do anything to see that she was fed and cared for."

I felt the Lord was telling me, "So would I. Why don't you ask Me to do something great to help these kids?" The impression was to ask big. Don't ask for truckloads or even trainloads of provisions, ask for cargo shiploads. There is plenty in heaven for them.

Of course, at that point, I had no budget or funds to help them. I remember asking the Lord just for funds to feed all of the kids I had seen that day for a whole year.

A day or two later, I had traveled to Japan and was speaking in a church where I shared the story of the graveyard. Unexpectedly, the pastor stopped the service to take up an offering. This wasn't a large church, but I never had seen the spirit of generosity fall on a congregation in that way. It was a move of the Holy Spirit. I later learned that some had left church to go to the ATM machine. People even followed us to the airport, putting envelopes in my hand as I went into the terminal.

After figuring the money exchange rate, I discovered not only were there enough funds to feed those kids for a year, but plenty to feed hundreds more. Beginning that year, with the offering I had received, our ministry started ten feeding programs in the Philippines to feed more than 1,000 kids for one year. This ministry has continued to grow since that day in 1999.

In pondering the trip and the ways I have seen God move since, I recalled a story of a minister who was visiting with some African pastors. He was deeply impacted by their joy and faith in God to provide, even though outwardly it seemed they had so little. One of them explained why they weren't worried about having enough for their needs: "O

> *Our God loves us, blesses us, and provides for us **plenty too much.***

brother! Our God loves us, blesses us, and provides for us **plenty too much**."

I loved that quote. It is the perfect way for me to encourage you, through this book, to look to Him. Together we will mine the incredible truths Jesus taught the world for switching our mindset from one of poverty to plenty too much.

Chapter 2

CHARLIE'S LUNCH

Then Jesus lifted up His eyes, and seeing a great multitude coming toward Him, He said to Philip, "Where shall we buy bread, that these may eat?" But this He said to test him, for He Himself knew what He would do. Philip answered Him, "Two hundred denarii worth of bread is not sufficient for them, that every one of them may have a little." One of His disciples, Andrew, Simon Peter's brother, said to Him, "There is a lad here who has five barley loaves and two small fish, but what are they among so many?" (John 6:5-9 NKJV).

As I mentioned, the simple faith of one child changed the lives of thousands. But what about the disciples? What was going on in their minds as the little boy brought his lunch?

We know in the story; the disciples had become very weary and overwhelmed by the crowds. Jesus had told them they were going to get away for a rest. But here they were surrounded by crowds that were hounding Jesus the way the paparazzi chases a movie star. They had wanted to send the crowd away. The disciples suggested to Jesus that He send the people to the towns to get food. But Jesus had another plan. He did something He loves to do. He challenged his followers to attempt the impossible. He said, "*You* give them something to eat."

Part of the inspiration for writing this book came from the story of a little boy in my own family that was a catalyst for a miracle God did with the offer of a simple lunch.

Charlie was my nephew. He lived with his family in Guatemala. Charlie was born with a serious heart defect and it was miraculous that he survived his first year. As the son of missionary parents, Charlie stood out because of his generous spirit. He would offer his toys and possessions freely to the many needy children who lived around them in Guatemala City. On his first day of kindergarten, he was excited to have his very own lunch to take to school. When he got home, his mom asked him about how he enjoyed his lunch. He told her he decided to give his lunch to Micah, a boy who didn't have one. Later, his mother was told that Charlie had the biggest smile on his face as he watched Micah eat.

At the age of twelve, Charlie's heart suddenly stopped and he passed into the arms of Jesus. The next months were rough, especially for his dad and mom, Sam and Janey Stewart.

One day, as the grief felt unbearable, Janey heard a knock on the door. Standing there was one of the children from the streets asking for food. Suddenly, Janey was prompted: "Why don't you give him the lunch you would've made for Charlie?" She did, and the next day the same boy showed up with his friends. That one lunch grew to four, then six, and, you guessed it, an ever-growing stream of kids. Through this event, Sam and Janey discovered a new calling that continues to this day, more than 20 years later. They began a ministry that helps local churches on the frontlines of poverty feed, educate, and disciple children for Christ. They named it, "Charlie's Lunch," a ministry currently rooted in six countries that has served approximately seven million meals, and has broken the weight of poverty over the lives of thousands of children and families.

They love to say, "Charlie's Lunch is so much more than a plate of food." It has been a doorway to move into the lives of families. There are over five generations that have passed through the program. Large numbers of those children are now serving other children through the ministry. Many churches have been planted through Charlie's Lunch. Only in heaven will we know the impact of this ministry, all rising out of the generosity and faith of one little child.

It is that spirit of faith and generosity that God wants to stir up in all of us. There is no limit to what God might accomplish through us the moment we are prepared to move from a mindset of "never enough" to "plenty too much." I challenge you to get ready to be stirred. God wants us to move from thinking like *paupers* to thinking like *partners* with Him in the distribution of His abundance.

> *There is no limit to what God might accomplish through us the moment we are prepared to move from a mindset of "never enough" to "plenty too much."*

APPLICATION

With the loss of Janey and Sam's son, grief was almost unbearable. Then came a knock at the door and an invitation to partner with God for miracles. Maybe you too are grieving, discouraged, or maybe it seems there is never enough; God is knocking at your/our heart's door.

Why not begin opening the door with a prayer to grow in faith and generosity that comes from Jesus's plenty too much love for you?

There is no limit to what God might accomplish in and through us the moment we move from a mindset of "never enough" to "plenty too much."

Chapter 3

WHAT IS A PLENTY TOO MUCH MINDSET?

"And Jesus said to them, "I am the bread of life.
He who comes to Me shall never hunger and he
who believes in Me shall never thirst"
                          (John 6:35 NKJV).

A plenty too much mindset is one in which we see, plan, and act based on what is in God's pocket, not ours. A popular series of Capital One credit card commercials always end with the question, "What's in your wallet?" This is a game-changing question to ask when we think of the riches we have in Christ.

To help the disciples switch their thinking, Jesus challenged them to partner with Him in achieving the impossible: the feeding of 5,000 men besides the women and children. Of course, Philip's mind went immediately to what he had instead of considering Whom he was with. This made him feel uptight, and possibly possessive of whatever little he and the disciples had in their backpacks. He was bound by

> *A plenty too much mindset is one in which we see, plan, and act based on what is in God's pocket, not ours.*

logic and memory that said this was impossible.

A plenty too much mindset sees another wallet. It sees the storehouse of heaven. It sees the One who is the bread (source/sufficiency) of life. If only we could truly see and believe that, we would have so much more peace and much less worry.

With an abundance mindset, we are not beggars but believers; we are not paupers but partners with God. He has given us the keys to the storehouse (Matt. 16:19). We believe as Isaiah 65:24 NIV says, *"Before they call, I will answer."* Try that on your cell phone. The idea is that, before the need, God has already planned the supply. Interestingly, Jesus was *"the Lamb who was slain from the foundation of the world"* (Rev. 13:8 NKJV). In other words, before there were sinners, there was already a Savior.

In explaining the nearness of God and the presence of His kingdom, Dallas Willard says that God is in the very atmosphere surrounding us, constantly acting and interacting and desiring to make Himself known to us. God's presence is not far away, but here and now, all around.[1]

God is available to us now and here. Even the veil of pain, problems and suffering doesn't put Him beyond our reach.

Jesus pointed that out when someone asked Him why a man was born blind. Rather than debating why he was born blind, He invited them to see from God's abundance perspective. He said that this had happened so that the works of God might be displayed in him (John 9:3). From an abundance perspective, Jesus would say that being born blind allows the works of God to be made manifest.

People with an abundance mindset believe that in every situation there is more, there is better and there is greater. They aren't relying on the past to dictate what is possible but are daring to ask God for the future that He says can be. They believe there is not just one solution, but many solutions and opportunities in every problem. They refuse to settle for what other people think is possible. When others say it can't be done, they are already on their way to doing it.

They know that every day, someone is doing something that others have said couldn't be done. When the world was saying man could never fly, the Wright brothers were building an airplane. While people were saying in the 1950s that it is humanly impossible for a man to run a mile in under four minutes, Roger Bannister was preparing to do it.

On a spiritual level, people with an abundance mindset could be described as having a passion for the fullness of God. They not only believe in theory that all things are possible with God (Mk.10:27), but refuse to be content with a status quo that doesn't validate that belief. In contrast, I heard a story about a man who dreamed he was in heaven. An angel took him on a tour of this massive warehouse where millions of beautifully wrapped gifts were on mile-high shelves.

"What are these?" the man asked.

The angel replied, "These are the gifts that God had prepared for His kids. They are opportunities, miracles, open doors, encounters with the Holy Spirit that were left on the shelf. This one was an opportunity for Mary to have the job of a lifetime. This was Johnny's anointing to change the lives of an entire city in Africa. But they never came to claim their packages."

People with a plenty too much mindset refuse to let lack be their legacy. In Ephesians 3, the apostle Paul prays for people to have their spiritual eyes open to the overwhelming abundance of God's love, purposes and power for them. In verse 19 (NKJV), he uses the phrase, *"...to know the love of Christ which passes knowledge; that you may be filled with the **fullness** of God."* In the following verses, Paul explodes in this plenty too much doxology: *"Now to Him who is able to do exceedingly abundantly above all that we ask or think, according to the power that works in us, to Him be the glory in the church by Christ Jesus to all generations, forever and ever."*

Wow! What I draw out of that is the word "fullness." It is a great word for abundance, or plenty too much thinking, in the Bible. He is teaching that all Jesus provided for us at the cross, and the sufficiency of who He presently is, should be an active part of our lives. A person with a passion for fullness doesn't compare their experience to what others say is possible, but to what *God* says is possible because of Jesus.

What drives them is a hunger for all God has for their lives. They aren't satisfied to merely *have* the Holy Spirit; they insist on being "filled with the Holy Spirit." In Ephesians 5:18, the word "filled" means to be saturated, overflowing, or oozing like a sponge that's just been soaked in water. People with a passion for fullness don't just ask the Lord to fill their cup. They expect the Holy Spirit to be a mighty river flowing out of them; a river that changes the atmosphere, bringing a sense of the glory of heaven to the circumstances of Earth (John 7:38).

In the natural, it would've been acceptable for Jesus to send the people away to scrounge for food. But Jesus had a passion to do more. He wanted to show them that heaven could invade Earth; that the Bread of heaven, Jesus Himself, who could always be with them and in them, was plenty too much for their needs. He wants more for you and me than we even want for ourselves. Remember, He is a plenty too much God who longs to be overly generous with His children.

> *He wants more for you and me than we even want for ourselves.*

This reminds me of the heart my wife has towards our grand-children. We have 18 grandkids and nothing can move their Grammy's heart faster than thinking of ways to love and spoil them. If it's the two of us, leftovers will always do. But if the grandkids are coming, there must be something more than the ordinary with which to bless them.

It was this kind of passion that Moses had in Exodus 33. God had told Moses He would send an angel to accompany them to the Promised Land. Many people would've said that sounds good, we will have what we need. But not Moses; his passion would not settle for anything less than God's full presence, His glory fully known and shining in his life. Moses prayed, *"If Your Presence does not go with us, do not send us up from here. How will anyone know that You are pleased with me and with Your people unless You go with us? What else will distinguish me and Your people from all the other people on the face of the Earth?"* The Lord answered Moses saying, *"I will do the very thing you have asked, because I am pleased with you and I know you by name"* (Exod. 33:15-17 NIV).

Moses went on to say, "Show me Your glory," referring to the weight and "Allness" of God fully revealed. God loved Moses's prayer and his passion for God's fullness. That is what set Moses apart and why he saw God do for and through him what had not been done through anyone up to that time. He believed there were always more and greater possibilities and refused to settle for less. This is how abundance people think and why they are different.

A.W. Tozer said, "Acute desire must be present or there will be no manifestation of Christ to His people. He waits to be wanted. Too bad that with many of us, He waits so long, so very long, in vain."[2]

Fullness in our life is not measured by what is available in God, but by what is passionately believed, expected and claimed in us.

My mother was one of those "plenty too much" people. Her passion for God's fullness, and the belief that it was her birthright, put her in position to witness miracles few see, and allowed her to pass down that legacy to her family and many others.

In 1982, she had been medically diagnosed with glaucoma, as well as severe environmental allergies that caused her constant pain. She also felt nearly suffocated when around fumes and was unable to be in sunlight without thick sunglasses. Yet she never stopped expecting her miracle.

As an act of faith, she and my dad traveled to a healing service in Southern California. Ten years before, in a service at the same place, Melodyland Christian Center of Anaheim, she had received a miracle healing in her back. She returned because she was reminded of the story of the four lepers in the Old Testament who sat on the outskirts of a city under siege. The entire city was desperate and at the point of starving, and being lepers, they knew they would be considered the most expendable. But they understood something that Mom also realized: faith is not passive. Faith is action; it steps out and takes a leap towards the unseen presence of God. In the words of the lepers, she said to herself, "Why sit here and die?" (2 Kings 7:3).

> *Faith is action; it steps out and takes a leap towards the unseen presence of God.*

It was a Thursday morning service and although in pain, she was enjoying the worship. The preacher said, "If you need healing today, don't look up here or anywhere else. Healing is in you because Jesus is in you."

While Mom wanted to believe it, her heart was crying out, "But Jesus, *pain* is in me."

Then she heard the Lord speak, "Oh, slow of heart to perceive, don't you know what you're feeling is Me. I'm in the pain."

She was confused but said, "Yes, Lord, I receive."

Mom recalled verses like 2 Corinthians 12:9 KJV, where Paul said, *"I will glory in my infirmities that the power of Christ may rest upon me."* The Hebrew children (Dan. 3) also came to her mind. They were in the fiery furnace, but Jesus was with them. So she said, "Yes, I embrace this. I glory that You are in this. You make darkness Your secret place (Ps. 18:11). Thank You, Lord, You are going to be fully revealed and glorified in this."

Suddenly, Jesus spoke to her and said, "Yes, I'm in the pain, but remember there is no pain in Me." The words were an explosion inside of her. In that moment, she knew He was all she needed for her situation and that a miracle healing had been made available to her. Instantly, all the pain in her lungs and the blurriness in her eyes were gone.

She walked from there into the sunlight without any sunglasses, giggling and rejoicing in God's power. My dad and brother urged her to put on her sunglasses, saying, "Look, we both really need ours."

She said, "No thank you."

She was rejoicing because she hadn't been able to see light like that in a long time. While they drove, the air conditioner happened to go out in the rental car. She was undaunted and rolled down the windows as she rode through the smog without coughing or irritation – which she would've struggled with even before developing her condition.

Later, when the doctors confirmed her healing with tests, they were astonished. Because of this miracle, Mom and

Dad were able to continue fulfilling their ministry for many years. She never again suffered from those afflictions. She lived the fullness of her calling because she believed God's provision was plenty too much.

APPLICATION

People with an abundance mindset ask God for the future He says can be.

Consider an area where you have settled for *status quo* instead of God's flow.

1. God has more but I have settled for the *status quo* in the area of_____ .

2. I plan to step into God's flow by _____ .
    (Share your plan with an accountability friend.)

God wants more for you and me than we even want for ourselves.

Chapter 4

HONEY, I SHRUNK THE LORD

"It would take more than half a year's wages..."
"...how far will they go among so many?"
(John 6:7-9 NIV).

*"Do not work for food that spoils, but for food that
endures to eternal life, which the Son of man will
give you"* (John 6:27 NIV).

In 1989, a movie came out called *"Honey, I Shrunk the
Kids"*. It was a funny movie about a dad who was con-
ducting a scientific experiment with a machine that could
shrink big objects into smaller sizes. He accidentally shrank
his children in the process. The movie went on to show how
he found his ant-sized children and used the machine to
change them back to their rightful size. This illustrates a
major problem that unbelief can cause. Many of us fail to
see the miracles God wants to produce in our lives because
mentally, we have "shrunk the Lord!"

Even the great Moses succumbed to this. In Numbers Chapter 11, we read a story not too dissimilar from the one we're studying in this book. The children of Israel came complaining to Moses because they were tired of the manna God was providing, and they wanted meat. As Moses prayed about this, God told him He was going to provide the million-plus people with meat the next day. So much, in fact, that they would have meat until it came out of their nostrils. (Numbers 11:20)

Moses' mind shut down over that thought. He said, *"Would they have enough if flocks and herds were slaughtered for them? Would they have enough if all the fish in the sea were caught for them?"* (verse 22 NIV).

The Lord's answer to Moses was, *"Is the Lord's arm too short?"* (verse 23 NIV) In other words, "Did you just shrink in your mind what My Almighty hand has power to do?" How often have we had a "too good to be true" attitude towards the promises of God? In the process, we've brought God's Word down to the level of our past experience, instead of letting our experience rise to the level of God's Word. In Psalms 78:41 NKJV, the writer described what Moses did here and what the people did on

> ...we've brought God's Word down to the level of our past experience, instead of letting our experience rise to the level of God's Word.

22

so many occasions, as limiting the Holy One of Israel. Yes indeed, Honey, they shrunk the Lord.

You've heard it said that it is easier to take the boy out of the slums than to take the slums out of the boy. There are all kinds of external forms of poverty we are called to combat, caused by things like injustice, natural disasters, wars, disease, and famine. But there are also inner forces of poverty waging war against us, hindering us not only from having God's best, but also from becoming poverty busters for others.

Unbelief is one example of what the Bible refers to as strongholds in our minds. Strongholds are mental locks and lids that shut down our faith, preventing us from receiving what God says can be ours. In her book, *Praying God's Word*, Beth Moore defines a stronghold as anything that exalts itself in our minds, "...pretending to be bigger or more powerful than our God."[3]

We may have an argument in our mind that is based on natural facts, but leads us to conclusions that are lies. When I was a child, I was very shy. I concluded that I could never be a public speaker, based on how nervous I felt every time I spoke in front of people. For several years, this thinking blocked God's power to use me to share His Word. In fact, the apostle James describes this kind of thinking as a wisdom from this world that may seem right and logical, but is in fact worldly, fleshly, and devilish (James 3:15). You may have believed lies like "I could never afford to tithe" or "I just couldn't share my faith with someone." These stem from the spirit of poverty. It's lies of unbelief that tell us "you will never have enough or be enough" to fulfill your potential and see God's power work mightily through your life.

The lie of religion tells us that God is only going to bless you according to your good works. Because of this lie, so many people are on a treadmill of religious performance, never believing they are worthy enough for God to bless or use their lives. The truth is that God relates to those in Christ not on the basis of their own righteousness, but on a worthiness that comes from what Jesus did for us on the cross. When people see this, a giant wall prohibiting their progress and victory is removed. They begin to approach God and live like favored sons, not as fearful and shame-filled slaves.

> *The key component of an abundant life is giving and adding value to others.*

The key component of an abundant life is giving and adding value to others. The lie of poverty tells us we must cling to what we have out of fear of not having enough. As someone said, we must "get all we can, can all we get, and sit on the can." This tragically stops the flow of God's blessing on our lives.

James Ryle said, "Poverty is not the lack of things, but the fear of lack that causes us to cling desperately to what we have." This thinking causes a cycle of poverty to take hold. I read about a village in India where natural disasters had wiped out several crops. The villagers began living in fear, even though they had been provided with emergency food. They were given truckloads of seed for growing crops. But instead of sowing the seed, out of fear, they ate the seed. You can imagine what happened by the next harvest: they ran out of food.

The poverty spirit not only applies to provision but to our potential; not only to the fear of not having enough, but also the fear of not being enough. Both flow from unbelief. The following paragraph describes this kind of thinking and its consequences:

> *Don't run, you might fall*
> *Don't love, you might not be loved in return*
> *Don't give, you might not have enough*
> *Don't laugh or cry, you might be misunderstood*
> *Don't share your convictions, you might offend*
> *Don't ask, the answer might be no*
> *Don't experiment, you might have to start over*
> *Don't expect, you might be disappointed*
> *Don't forgive, you might get hurt again*
> *Don't dream, it might not happen*
> *Don't live, you might die.*[4]

The truth is that, although you might fall, and you might have to start over again, or you might be rejected, every step against the tide of fear is a seed of faith. In each attempt, you grow your faith muscles and plant a seed to see God do bigger things, and bring bigger breakthroughs which, in turn, cause you to have faith to think bigger and see bigger results, unleashing a cycle of prosperity and victory.

Poverty can take another form as well: the lie of "materialism" (what someone called the *assumption of consumption*). This is the mindset that clinging to things will make you happy and prosperous. Jesus warned over and over about a "spirit of mammon," that idolizes material gain and shrinks the heart of joy and contentment. Jesus tells us that life does not merely consist of the abundance of things you possess. Some have taken the principles of faith and misapplied them to create a false materialistic definition of success and prosperity. This is sometimes referred to as the "prosperity gospel." Great faith should always be defined in terms of what we give, not what we get.

I like the definition of prosperity given by one of my dearest mentors, Wayne Myers. This is a man who lives very modestly, a missionary for nearly 70 years, who has personally given away millions of dollars. He could've easily funneled people's generosity to his personal gain, but because he understands true prosperity, he has shunned that mentality to live a life of sacrifice for others. He teaches that prosperity isn't about having more for us, but is about building bigger channels for God to flow *through* us to others. He defines prosperity this way:

"For me prosperity is going to sleep at night without sleeping pills and having all of my investments in a heavenly bank account where the interest rates are three, six, and then a thousand percent. Prosperity is bringing souls into the kingdom, and seeing my tiny seed grow into productive lives all around the globe. God's prosperity is having your own needs met with enough left over to bless others in need."[5]

When the people came to Jesus the following day looking for more bread, He told them that the bread they were seeking couldn't satisfy their souls; that He Himself is the Bread of Life. You might say true prosperity isn't what you *possess*, but what possesses *you*.

If you are growing in your relationship with Jesus and living to give, you are rich and are going to be full of joy no matter what you have or don't have on the outside. If you are looking to things, you will be empty and disappointed, no matter what you have on the outside.

This poem on poverty beautifully exposes the fallacy of materialism:

POVERTY IS

Poverty is untested potential and unused opportunities.

Poverty is having a dishwasher, two cars, the latest TV but anxiously looking forward to going somewhere and get away from it all.

Poverty is spending your whole life working at a job you don't like so you can someday retire and do what you want.

Poverty is having a roomful of presents on Christmas or your birthday, and then being completely bored the next day because there is nothing to do.

Poverty is buying things you don't need, with money you don't have, to impress people you don't like.

Poverty is having many acquaintances but no true friends.

Poverty is rushing through life and never having time to stop and drink in the beauty of God's glory all around you.

Poverty is being lonely in a crowd of people, talking and not feeling you are heard.

Poverty is being around God but never having an intimate relationship with Him.

Poverty is gaining the whole world and losing your soul.[6]

Pastor Mark Pfeifer does an excellent job defining a spirit of poverty in his book, *Breaking the Spirit of Poverty*. He says:

> "People who labor under a yoke of poverty feel smaller than other people most of the time. Sometimes it compels them to overachieve while at other times the spirit of poverty causes people to underachieve. For this reason, a spirit of poverty cannot be found in what someone has received, but in what they have given away. The spirit keeps people from dreaming dreams, taking risks and releasing to others. They live in fear of losing what they have so they grasp every form of treasure that they own. They have a difficult time giving away love, compliments, friendships and money."

> "People living under a spirit of poverty never feel strong enough to survive. They don't feel smart enough to succeed, fortunate enough to catch a break, loved enough to be secure, nice enough to be friends, prosperous enough to get ahead and wealthy enough to give to others. This sense of lack creates fear, which convinces them to bury their talent and treasure. To these people, not losing is winning, not giving up ground is progress; not dying is living and not failing is succeeding."

> "A spirit of poverty has robbed God's people so deeply of His blessings that we have come to expect lack in our

families and congregations. We think it is normal not to have enough. We think it's normal to be in debt over our head and unable to fulfill the vision of the church because there are insufficient funds." [7]

As you read this, I wonder if there are ways you have allowed this spirit to affect you. My friend, is there a place in your life today where you have shrunk the Lord?

APPLICATION

The poverty spirit not only applies to the fear of not having enough, but also, the fear of not being enough. A poverty spirit shrinks the Lord and robs us of many blessings.

Try rephrasing the following "poverty" thoughts into Jesus possibilities.

1 • If only I had the talent/education/personality they have.
2 • If anything can go wrong, it will.
3 • If I try and fail, what will people think?
4 • I will give when I have enough.
5 • Now, my whole day is ruined.
6 • It's too late; if only I had known.

If you are growing in your relationship with Jesus and living to give, you are rich...

God created us Successful—
God's Plan
God's Purpose

Chapter 5

SUCCESS IS WHO YOU ARE

P eople not only struggle with the belief they will never have enough, a spirit of poverty also seeks to convince them they will never *be* enough. I call them strongholds of a false self-image, lies that come from seeing ourselves through the prism of other people's opinions. Lids of low self-esteem are pervasive in people's lives today. For example, in a survey, eighty-four percent of women said they felt unattractive. It is crucial that we learn how to look at the picture of ourselves that's in God's wallet and not ours.

Author Zig Ziglar said, "You cannot consistently perform in a manner that is inconsistent with the way you see yourself."[8] We see this in the children of Israel who refused to enter the Promised Land that God said was already theirs to possess. In their own words, they describe themselves in comparison to the giants of the land: *"We were like grasshoppers in their eyes"* (Numbers 13:33 NIV). In their perception of the challenges before them, they saw themselves weak as bugs.

> *...to some degree, every person wears an invisible crown of favor and self-esteem..., or an invisible chip of "not enough"..., depending on how they perceive themselves.*

I believe that, to some degree, every person wears an invisible crown of favor and self-esteem on their head, or an invisible chip of "not enough" on their shoulder, depending on how they perceive themselves.

I saw this displayed as I was trying to help a young person who said she just couldn't make any friends at school or church. I talked to my daughter, Heidi, who was about the same age and had an abundance of friends. I was hoping that she might suggest a few techniques to help this girl.

I asked "Heidi, how do you get so many friends?"

She said, "Oh, Dad, I don't try to get friends. I just know everyone wants to be my friend."

I realized her confidence and ability to attract friends came not from who she was trying to be in others' eyes, but who she knew she already was in God's eyes.

I remember hearing the example of a Jewish mother. In their community, children are raised to see themselves having a certain future.[9] When asked the names of her 3-and 5-year-old sons, the mother said, "This is my lawyer David and my doctor Reuben." It isn't surprising that these children pursued professional careers.

An old saying goes: "You can't fly like an eagle if you think of yourself as a chicken."

There is a story of a farmer who found an egg that had fallen from an eagle's nest. He took it home and put it in his chicken coop for the hens to keep warm. The little eaglet hatched, but because all she ever saw were chickens, she developed her identity as a chicken. She always felt an urge to fly and that she was made for more, but her brain told her she was just a chicken, so she never tried. She learned to peck, scratch, and squawk, but wondered why she didn't fit in. One day, she saw an eagle soaring above the chicken coop and felt something awaken within her. Knowing her history, one of the old hens said, "Maybe that's your mother. You know you're an eagle, don't you? Go look at yourself in the water trough." Sure enough, the mirrored image confirmed that she was indeed different. So, she went out and lifted her eyes to see the eagles soaring above. As the wind blew under her wings, she took flight, joining her new companions. She never returned to the chicken coop.

Recently, I felt the Lord gave me a word for our church that I believe is for you as well, "It's time for the eagles to fly." You've lived in the nest of insecurity and low self-esteem long

> *You are an eagle, my friend. Dare to be yourself in Christ. Dare to fly!*

enough. You are an eagle, my friend. Dare to be yourself in Christ. Dare to fly!

In the Bible, in story after story, when God called someone to their destiny, He would change their name. He helped them see that destiny, success and victory must begin with who you are. So, then Abram became Abraham, meaning father of a multitude (Gen. 17:4-5). He didn't first have children and *then* come to be called a father of a multitude. He first was called a father of a multitude and *then* had children. Gideon, the "runt of his tribe and family, hiding in a cellar from the enemy" was suddenly greeted by an angel who announced his identity, *"The Lord is with you, mighty warrior"* (Judg. 6:12 NIV). Simon became Peter the rock, upon which Jesus said He would build His church (Matt. 16:18). I believe that the Holy Spirit is constantly trying to make clear the reputation God has put on us; the way we're already seen in heaven. *Be silent & listen*

God is waiting for us to call out what He sees in us. On an episode of the *700 Club* program, Gordon Robertson quoted from a psychological study suggesting that eighty percent of the self-talk of an average American (what we say about ourselves) is negative.[10] There is power in the tongue, even of life and death (Prov. 18:21). No wonder there are so many discouraged people.

We seem to have the ability to talk ourselves out of God's favor and blessing. Yet, the Bible says David "... encouraged

'Be mindful of my words'

himself in the Lord" (1 Sam. 30:6 KJV). He agreed with God's assessment of him and spoke blessing and favor over his life. When David stood before Goliath, the giant tried to convince David that he was worthless and weak. But David wouldn't have it, boldly declaring that he was in covenant with God, and could do what *God* said he could do. This empowered him to overwhelm the giant (I Sam. 17:43-46). I believe God is pleased when we speak positively to and about ourselves; when we affirm our progress and believe confidently in who we are in Christ.

It was said that John G. Lake, one of the most powerful evangelists of the last century, had a daily routine of looking in the mirror before he left for work and declaring "God is going to work in that man's suit."

Again, my mother had an experience that defined her life. One day she walked into the bathroom and when she looked in the mirror, saw a vision of Jesus looking at her. She was stunned and asked the Lord what that meant. He spoke to her that this is how He saw her. He saw the righteousness of Christ, and the person of Christ living through her.

James also talks about someone who looked in a mirror. In James 1:23-24, he describes a man "who looked at his face in the mirror, and after seeing himself, goes away and immediately forgets what he looks like." James explains that this is someone who looks into God's Word–the Bible. He reads about his new identity and how he is now able to and should live, but doesn't do anything about it. He doesn't put actions to his beliefs.

Do:

To break a spirit of poverty off our self-esteem and identity, we must not just passively hear about our new identity in Christ. We have to deliberately begin to act in faith on that identity. Gideon rose up, tore down the family idol and recruited an army to fight because he was acting on his belief that he was a mighty warrior (Judg. 6-7). David charged a giant because he believed the word of Samuel that he was anointed to reign (1 Sam. 17). Our identity is established when we internalize the truth of who we are in Christ to the point of action. Victorious people don't just believe they are champions, they get in the ring and get some wins under their belt, by acting in faith upon the truth of their new identity.

> *Victorious people don't just believe they are champions, they get in the ring and get some wins under their belt*

As a young man, I felt called to be an evangelist but had great insecurity about whether God would really use me. The call could've just been an idea that I left on the shelf. But I received an unusual opportunity to give the message and altar call at a huge evangelistic event that involved a famous Christian rock band. Hundreds of people filled the stadium, which was hewn into the rock-face of a famous canyon of our city. I frantically toiled over what I would say. But as I sat in the stadium about to speak, I sensed the

Holy Spirit clearly tell me to ditch what I had prepared. This terrified me. I sensed that God wanted to challenge me. He wanted me to minister based on my identity and not my ability. Would I believe what He had told me about being an evangelist, or would I try to prove that I was a good enough preacher to be an evangelist?

So, it truly was with fear and trembling that I stood on the platform, affirming to God that I hadn't chosen this, He was the One who called me and told me I was an evange-list. I trusted Him to come through as I stepped into the shoes of faith, that I was who He said I was and could do what He said I could do. That night, the words did come and there was a huge response to the altar call. As I took a step of faith, my true identity was no longer just a theory – it was a reality.

Let me ask, who do you see when you look in the mirror? What are you doing to establish in your heart the true knowledge of who you really are and to no longer believe the lies of who you once thought you were?

APPLICATION

When you look at yourself in the mirror, who you see will affect how you respond in life and those around you. All of us feel insecure about something, sometime. How we respond is a choice.

1. When I feel insecure, I feel like
    a. Staying in the nest.
    b. Running to the chicken coop.
    c. Squawking like a hen.
    d. Flying like an eagle.

2. Describe what it means to fly like an eagle. What area would you like to dare to be yourself and fly?

You are an eagle, my friend. Dare to be yourself in Christ. Dare to fly!

To fly like an eagle means to soar above your established capabilities/beliefs.

Chapter 6

I AM WHO HE SAYS I AM

"I am the bread of life. Whoever comes to Me will never go hungry, and whoever believes in Me will never be thirsty" (John 6:35 NIV).

"I am the living bread that came down from heaven. Whoever eats this bread will live forever. This bread is My flesh, which I will give for the life of the world" (John 6:51 NIV).

They say Disneyland is the magic kingdom. Certainly, people go there expecting fun and excitement. But who thinks of going to Disneyland to have a life-transforming encounter with Jesus? I know that sounds a little strange, but it happened when I was 19 years old. I was attending Melodyland School of Theology, across the street from Disneyland. From time to time, I would tag along with friends or take guests there for fun or vacation. But this day, I just couldn't get into the rides and magic. I was struggling, wondering deep inside if I even had what it took to be a Christian. I had experienced God's love in salvation, but I mostly felt condemned, inadequate, and like a failure. Temptations were regularly getting the best of me.

I can relate to the hungry people in our story who came looking for Jesus the next day. They had seen a miracle and had been physically fed. But like everything else in life, things of this world only gave temporary satisfaction. In John 6, Jesus so beautifully leads them to see something so much greater than what He gave to them physically. He showed them what He wanted to be for them. He said, *"I am the bread of life. Whoever comes to Me will never go hungry, and whoever believes in Me will never thirst."* He said *"I am the living bread that came down from heaven. Whoever eats this bread will live forever. This bread, is My flesh, which I give for the life of the world."*

Jesus reveals the message behind the miraculous sign. To the people of that day, bread represented sustenance. For the years the Hebrew children were in the wilderness, it was that bread that kept them alive. Here, Jesus is saying that all of those miracles pointed to something deeper: through His work at the cross and the outpouring of the Holy Spirit, He would not only offer forgiveness of sin, but His very life inside of us. He said He would be our source of life, our all in all. Jesus doesn't just promise to help improve our life; He is willing to do something so much greater. He is willing

> *He doesn't just promise to help improve our life.... He is willing to replace our life with His.*

to replace our life with His. Paul would describe this as the mystery which was hidden from the ages but has now been revealed: "Christ in you the hope of glory" (Col. 1:27).

In 2 Corinthians 8:9 NLT, Paul said, *"Though He was rich, yet for your sakes He became poor, so that by his poverty He could make you rich."* The wealth he is speaking of is the sufficiency of Christ living His life through us. In Philippians 4:13 NKJV, Paul referred to this truth by saying, *"I can do all things through Christ who strengthens me."* The Amplified Version emphasizes that He fuses His very strength with our lack of strength to make us complete and sufficient. Paul discovered what it meant not just to live for Christ but **from** Christ and as Christ living in him.

I remember reading about a fellow walking through a field and seeing what appeared to be a man tirelessly pumping a well. The man seemed to never stop, slow down or even get tired. As the traveler drew closer he saw that it wasn't a man at all. It was a scarecrow, who had a wooden arm with a swivel attached to the handle of a pump. The pump actually channeled an artesian well springing up from the ground. The man wasn't pumping the well, the well was pumping the man! That is what it means to live from Christ, not just for Christ.

That day at Disneyland, I decided to journey to Tom Sawyer's Island. There I lay in a wooded area, crying out to the Lord to show me "Who am I? What am I supposed to do? How can I change and become the person you want me to be?"

Suddenly, it was like the Holy Spirit opened the eyes of my heart and made it so clear to me. A verse I had memorized came to mind. *"I have been crucified with Christ and I no longer live, but Christ lives in me. The life I now live in the body, I live by faith in the Son of God, who loved me and gave Himself for me"* (Gal. 2:20 NIV).

It just hit me that I didn't need to figure out who I was to become, I was to realize who I already was in union with Christ. God didn't intend for me to become *something* but simply to contain *Someone*, who was already in me and for me and wanted to be all I needed. I didn't need to be improved; I was already replaced. Christ in me was way more than enough strength, self-control, love, wisdom, peace, and joy. He reminded me of how I hadn't chosen Him, but He had chosen me, as the branch through which He, the Vine, would bear much fruit (John 15:5). I only needed to learn how to partake of what I already had inside of me.

> *Christ in me was way more than enough strength, self-control, love, wisdom, peace, and joy.*

That turned a switch from poverty to abundance in my thinking and experience. It isn't that I became perfect. I am still so very weak and inadequate in myself to this day. It is just that I saw, in my weakness I was at my strongest because God's strength was available and accessible to flow through me (2 Cor. 12:9-10). I became aware of who HE is in me. I remember that day feeling as though Jesus were looking through my eyes, touching through my hand, and speaking through my voice, because He was in me but I had not realized it. I learned experientially that I had a source I could draw from.

I began to recognize the difference between my soul and spirit. My soul is where my feeling, reasoning, and memory lie. My spirit is the real me, who lives in union with Christ. Just like I have a shirt that I'm wearing, but the real me is not a shirt. I have feelings, beliefs, memories, and thoughts from my old self but I am not them. I have learned that I can step into the awareness of who Jesus is in me by agreeing and partnering with what He says, while putting aside the old feelings and actions of my old self. I can cast those off, the way I throw away a bill that's been paid, as something irrelevant and powerless.

Declarations of scripture have helped me claim and remember who I really am. Below are some samples of those scriptures.

Declarations:

1. I am not a sinner trying to be more holy. I am the righteousness of God, putting off my old self and living in

agreement with my new nature that loves righteousness and hates sin. *2 Cor. 5:21, Eph. 4:22-24*

2. I am not an orphan or a beggar in God's kingdom. I am a son/daughter – a beloved, chosen, royal ruling child of God in whom He delights and sings over every day. *I John 3:1, Eph. 1:4-7, Zeph. 3:17, I Pet. 2:9, Rev. 5:10*

3. I am not a sick person who hopes to get well, I am a whole and healthy person in Christ standing against sickness and disease. I believe the same power that raised Jesus from the dead is able to give life, healing and strength to my mortal body. *Isa. 53:5, I Pet. 2:24, Eph.1:18-21, Col. 2:10, Rom. 8:11*

4. I have failed but I am not a failure. I am a righteous person who rises and learns from failure and who is growing in grace and knowledge of who I really am. I am well able to overcome, I am dead to sin, I am more than a conqueror through Christ who strengthens me. In fact, it is no longer I who live, but Christ who lives in me. *Gal. 2:20, Rom. 8:35-37, 2 Pet. 3:18, Rom. 6:11*

5. I am a hilariously, unreasonably positive and joyful person who loves to give, and is more blessed every time I have a chance to give, than when I receive. God makes all grace abound toward me so that, having all sufficiency in all things, I abound and am generous in

giving good things and doing good works on any occasion. *Acts 20:35, 2 Cor. 9:8, Eph. 2:10*

6. The same power that raised Jesus from the dead lives in me. I have been appointed to do the works that Jesus did and greater works, because He is praying for me and has given me His Holy Spirit. I expect miracles, breakthroughs, and signs and wonders to accompany me every time I share the Good News of Jesus Christ. *Rom. 8:11, John 14:12, Mark 16:17-18, John 17:20-23, Heb. 7:25, John 16:7*

7. God is meeting all of my needs, not according to the economy I live in, but according to his riches in glory. I have wisdom, skills, and favor to adequately see all of my family's needs addressed with plenty in reserve to help others. *Phil. 4:19, I Cor. 1:30, Rom. 12:6-8*

8. I believe I have plenty too much confidence, because Scripture says I can do all things through Christ who releases His strength in me. *Phil. 4:13, Eph. 3:12*

9. I believe I can confidently make great decisions, because I have the mind of Christ, and Jesus has become my wisdom, sanctification, and righteousness. *I Cor. 1:30, I Cor. 2:16*

10. I believe and declare that Christ in me is the hope of glory for my life, my family, and those He has called me to influence. *Col. 1:27*

11. Because Christ is my life, I am now able to be a partaker of the divine nature in each and every situation I face. *2 Pet. 1:3-4*

Jesus clearly modeled for us how to help others out of poverty into an abundant lifestyle. In these next chapters, we will explore what this story teaches us about helping others.

APPLICATION

"Who am I? What am I supposed to do? How can I change and become the person God wants me to be?" These age-old questions have *Jesus* answers.

To begin the process of discovering the answers, try speaking the above declarations over yourself, look up scriptures, or write a declaration on a card and memorize.

You are who He says you are!

Chapter 7

LOVE IS THE KEY

*"When Jesus landed and saw a large crowd, He
had compassion on them and healed their sick. As
evening approached, the disciples came to Him and
said, "This is a remote place, and it's getting late.
Send the crowds away, so they can go to the villages
and buy themselves some food."*
*Jesus replied, "They do not need to go away. You give
them something to eat"* (Matt. 14:14-16 NIV).

W e have seen thus far, the important role faith
played in breaking the spirit of poverty and
releasing a miracle. But there was something more. There
was a power behind Jesus's faith that drove this miracle. It
was the power of love. The Scriptures say when Jesus saw
the large crowds, He had compassion on them. Galatians
5:6 NIV says, *"The only thing that counts is faith expressing
itself through love".* For those whose hearts are moved and
burdened by love to help others, we can fully expect that He
will always give faith to powerfully provide. Love and faith

are power twins. If we let our hearts be moved by love, great exploits of faith will follow.

I love the prayer made famous by Bob Pierce, the founder of World Vision, an organization that has changed the lives of millions in poverty. He prayed, "Lord, break my heart with the things that break yours."[11] I believe He was praying for the same stirring to happen in His heart that happened in Jesus's heart when he saw the multitudes.

Part of the World Vision story took place on an evangelistic trip to China. Bob led chapel at a girls' school. At a chapel service the next day, Tena, the principal, introduced Bob to White Jade, a child who had been abandoned for receiving Jesus.

"Well, you'll take care of her, won't you?" Bob asked Tena.

Tena answered, "The question isn't what I am going to do. The question is what are *you* going to do?"

Bob's heart was deeply moved with compassion to support the child. Eventually, the first child-sponsorship program was started as a response, a program that has helped hundreds of thousands of children over the years.[12]

I believe that before God moves mountains, He moves hearts with compassion. Those who change the world are not those who have the most or know the most, but those who love the most. These people discover that love is addictive and contagious. They begin giving as they live, but end up living to give.

This is the story of Wayne Myers, whom I introduced in Chapter 4, a ninety-seven-year-old champion of an abundance lifestyle. As mentioned, he is a missionary who has lived in Mexico for more than 70 years, living by faith, never asking for money, and yet being a channel through which millions of dollars, miracles, mercies and messages of hope flow.

Those who change the world are not those who have the most or know the most, but those who love the most.

One simple event took place in a little café in a small town in southern Mexico, where Wayne took a few of us to eat. It was a picture of "living to give", which he says is the motto of his life.

After we ate, he told us he was going to pay for dinner but asked if we were ready for the offering. I wasn't sure what he meant but we all gave some money for the "offering", which turned out to be the tip, and that is one of his favorite rituals when eating out. He called the waitress over and gave her the tip, an amount more than double the bill. She began to cry and the next thing we knew, he was praying for her and she was inviting the other restaurant staff over for a blessing. At that meal, he revealed that he had been told many times he would go broke living this way. I loved his comment, he said, "I was broke when I started to live like this 70 years ago, but I've never been broke since!"

The question to consider is, "What motivates this kind of love?" When I asked Wayne, he told me about how good and faithful Jesus had been to him, how as a sailor during WWII he found Christ and was forgiven of all of his sins. It reminded me of the woman who had come to Jesus and broken her expensive vase of perfume to wash His feet. Jesus explained that, because she had been forgiven much, she loved much *(Luke 7:47)*.

> *...what breaks the spell of materialism, selfishness, anger and unforgiveness is a personal revelation of God's overwhelming love for us.*

I believe what breaks the spell of materialism, selfishness, anger and unforgiveness is a personal revelation of God's overwhelming love for us. I believe everything changes and a spirit of poverty is broken when we discover something so much greater than earthly treasure. The reality is: we are God's treasure. When the Holy Spirit reveals the depth of God's personal love for us, the power of greed is broken.

Wayne likes to say, "I've known people who squeezed a dollar bill so tight, they made George Washington cry." Yet, the moment they realized how much Jesus loves them, their heart not only overflowed, their wallet and their bank account flowed with love and generosity as well.

This same love overwhelms our fear. I John 4:18 NKJV says, *"Perfect love casts out fear."* One of the questions I often ask is, "What if we weren't afraid anymore?" What if we weren't afraid to share Jesus with people because our love for them mattered more than their opinion of us? What if we were willing to go places God called us that are way outside of our comfort zone, because it mattered more to us that people were cared for than being comfortable?

A short time ago, my daughter Heidi wrote a blog titled, "What if we weren't afraid anymore?" I have cherished that article because of what I've seen happen in her life. Heidi, her husband Chris and their four boys are missionaries in Zambia. What amazes me is what that represents. In the natural, she might have been the last one of our six children that I would've imagined becoming a missionary. Growing up, she struggled with anxiety disorders and many illnesses. But her heart was moved by God in a powerful way on a mission trip as a teenager. She got a revelation of God's love for her and for people who live in poverty.

She has become as bold as a lion. Not because of her personality but because of a compassion and love bigger than any fear.

Another kind of fear is the worry Jesus addressed in His Sermon on the Mount, when He urged people not to worry about tomorrow. In particular, He spoke of the worry that we would not be able to make it on our everyday income. Jesus makes the point that we must realize and gratefully affirm how much the heavenly Father loves and cares for us. He emphasizes how much He cares for even the birds of the air and the lilies of the field, reminding us that we are so much more important to Him than they are. Even the hairs of our head are all numbered by Him (Matt. 6:26-34; Matt. 10:30-31).

He basically says that you've never heard of a sparrow on high blood pressure medicine or the lilies of the field stressing and having a meltdown about whether the sun will rise. One of my favorite verses to address this fear is Romans 8:32 NIV: *"He who did not spare His only Son but gave Him up for us all – how will He not also, along with Him, graciously give us all things?"* Worry is dissolved by realizing Father's great love.

I've imagined the scene of a 7-year-old boy sitting on the curb when his Dad drives up. His head is buried in his hands. When his Dad asks, "What's wrong?" the little boy says, "Oh, Dad! Have you noticed the price of milk lately? Dad, our monthly rent is pretty high, and the stock market may go bad today." That would break your heart as a parent. How much more does our heavenly Father want us to live the abundant, fun life He has planned for us and not waste life worrying.

So how do we come into a greater and greater realization of God's love for us? How can we let His love move us to faith, peace, and compassion? Here are three suggestions:

First, spend time asking the Holy Spirit to help you grasp God's unconditional love for you. Realize God doesn't love you because you are good, God loves you because He is love. I like a cute Dennis the Menace cartoon I read some time ago:

Dennis and Joey are leaving Mrs. Wilson's house with some delicious cookies she has given them.

"Dennis, why does Mrs. Wilson give us cookies? We're not good," Joey says.

"Oh, silly! Mrs. Wilson doesn't give us cookies because we're good. She gives us cookies because *she* is good," Dennis replies.[13]

God's love never changes. Nothing we could do could make Him love us more and nothing we can do would make Him love us less. He settled once and for all the degree of His love for us by what Jesus did for us

> *Nothing we could do could make Him love us more and nothing we can do would make Him love us less.*

on the cross. I remember one of those times when God was reminding me of His love for *me*. I was sitting in the back seat of our car as my parents were driving us home from California. My parents broke into singing this old hymn, *"The Love of God."* As I heard it, I was broken with the sense God was singing directly to my soul. It not only moved me towards God, but towards flowing in the love of God for others more than ever before. As you read the lyrics, why not ask the Lord to do something similar for you?

Love of God

The love of God is greater far
Than tongue or pen can ever tell;
It goes beyond the highest star,
And reaches to the lowest hell;
The guilty pair, bowed down with care,
God gave His Son to win;
His erring child He reconciled,
And pardoned from his sin.

Refrain:
O love of God, how rich and pure!
How measureless and strong!
It shall forever more endure.
The saints and angels' song.

Could we with ink the ocean fill,
And were the skies of parchment made.

Were every stalk on Earth a quill,
And every man a scribe by trade;
To write the love of God above
Would drain the ocean dry;
Nor could the scroll contain the whole;
Though stretched from sky to sky.[14]

Second, intentionally choose to quit trying to earn God's love by your works. We never become insecure about our position in our Father's love because He withholds it, but because we try and earn it.

I remember a time as a young Christian going to the desert after a week of stumbling into some frustrating habitual sins. In a dramatic way, I told the Lord that I thought He should just let me die and go home. I didn't want to backslide. But it seemed that no matter how hard I tried, I just wasn't good enough to be a Christian. As I prayed, my heart went back to the cross, and the realization that *that* was the very reason He died. Because I could never be good enough, He wanted to make a way for me to live in the full measure of His love. I literally felt baptized in love there, lying in the sand. I took note that, when I felt I deserved it the least, that was when He wanted to help me experience it the most. We like to say the news of the gospel is, "We are much worse in ourselves than we ever imagined, but so much more loved by Jesus than we could ever dream!"

Third, intentionally decide to make Jesus your treasure. One of the ways selfishness and poverty loses its grip is when what we treasure in Jesus truly becomes more important than anything we treasure on Earth. Jesus said, *"Where your treasure is, there your heart will be also"* (Matt 6:21 NIV). When you intentionally treasure Jesus in worship, sur-render, and obedience, your heart follows into being filled with His love and being free from the after-effects of your sinful nature.

We can, of course, treasure Jesus by worshipping Him. But one of the most powerful ways to treasure Jesus and be filled with the revelation of His love is to intentionally see Jesus in others and love them as an act of worship to Him, whether or not the persons seem to deserve it.

It's been said that when someone told Mother Teresa how wonderful it was that she'd been called to minister to the poor, she replied, "No, I haven't been called to minister to the poor, I've been called to pour my love on Jesus. It just so happens I have found Him among the poor."

What happens as we pour out our love on Jesus by loving others, we become changed. You can't be "Jesus with skin on" to other people in need, without more of His love taking over your heart and life.

APPLICATION

Compassion motivated Bob Pierce to help an abandoned child. Heidi overcame fear because love was bigger than her fear. A waitress was blessed by love and invited her friends to join the blessing.

1. Ask the Holy Spirit to help you grasp God's unconditional love for you. Fill in the blanks with words that describe God's never-changing, plenty too much, endless, perfect love.

I am disappointed in myself. God's love for me is

_____ .

I try to do my best. God's love for me is

_____ .

I serve the poor. God's love for me is

_____ .

I sin, fail, make a mess. God's love for me is

_____ .

2. Because He loves you, intentionally see Jesus loving and valuing the people you meet and pass-by every day. Name some ways you could show value to someone in the crowd.

The love of God is greater far than tongue or pen can ever tell... [15]

Chapter 8

An Unlikely Partner
For A Miracle

"Here is a boy with five small barley loaves and two small fish, but how far will they go among so many?" (John 6:9 NIV).

"As evening approached, the disciples came to him and said, this is a remote place, and it's already getting late. Send the crowds away, so they can go to the villages and buy themselves some food" (Matt. 14:15, NIV).

What I love about this story is that it teaches us how to partner with God for miracles. We all need miracles. Today in some area of your life – health, relationships, finances – you need a miracle. The great thing is that God *loves* to do miracles. Mark 10:27 says all things are possible with God. However, the miracle we want Him to do for us is often a miracle He wants to do *through* us. Maybe the miracle you are praying for God to do in your marriage is a miracle He wants to do *through you* in your marriage.

This especially applies to the miracles needed by the world around us. I heard the story about a couple of street boys starving in a slum. One boy said, "If God really loved us, He would have given us food and a place to stay. I don't think He

...the miracle we want Him to do for us is often a miracle He wants to do through us.

cares." The other boy said, "Yes, God does care, and I know He gave someone food to give us, but I think they just forgot to come."

The disciples were doing what we often do when a miracle is needed. They weren't acknowledging a miracle was needed nor did they ask the Miracle Giver for help. The gospels say by the time they mentioned it to Jesus it was late in the day. The Bible says, "You have not because you ask not" (James 4:2). How many of us are acknowledging our needs or asking God to do something about the needs around us? Are we waiting for somebody else to see and act?

Perhaps they were thinking, "What's wrong with these people? Are they depending on us to feed them?" You can also hear anxiety in their words, "What are we going to do?" Isn't it strange but so much like us? Here they have Jesus Christ, the King of kings, standing right in front of them and they're trying to figure out what they're going to do for lunch. But in the middle of their dilemma, Jesus shocks them with an unexpected directive:

"*You* feed them."

In other words, you take responsibility for this miracle happening. Have you ever had God ask you to do something impossible? Miracle faith only comes and grows when you are asking and attempting the impossible. It is clear why Jesus was asking them to do this. John 6:6 says He asked this to test them, for He already had in mind what He was going to do.

> When the Lord asks you to put your arms around an elephant, it is because He is about to grow your arms.

Faith grows when you are attempting what is not humanly possible. When the Lord asks you to put your arms around an elephant, it is because He is about to *grow* your arms. Some of you are being challenged to step out and attempt things for God that are financially and logically impossible. Congratulations! You are in miracle territory.

I believe He so wanted to use this situation to teach them how to look into God's pockets for the needs of the multitudes. He wanted them to see what He saw: lost sheep in desperate need of Jesus, the Bread of Life. Too often we tend to retreat from the overwhelming spiritual needs of the masses into the safer confines of our little group.

It is easier to dwell on the needs within the four walls of our church than to see a city or nation as our responsibility. How desperately the world needs Christians to come into a new faith for evangelism. When John Wesley saw the multitudes, he began to go outside the church and preach in the fields. He is famous for saying, "The world is my parish."[16]

Jesus has called us to be "fishers of men" (Matt. 4:19), but it is often easier to be keepers of the aquarium—to focus on the spiritual needs of our small group, or maintain our programs. I believe there is no area that more urgently needs an abundance mindset than evangelism. This is an area His heart longs for us to see, believe, and attempt the impossible.

> *Jesus has called us to be "fishers of men", but it is often easier to be keepers of the aquarium...*

It is so easy for lids and lies to block our vision. That is why so few are taking the challenge to pray Psalms 2:8, "Give us the nations for our inheritance." But what if those barriers for reaching the multitudes are not as big as they seem? What if in faith we believe that God could do something miraculous to multiply our gifts and efforts to feed thousands? What if God is waiting for us to step out in bold new ways to claim our cities for Christ?

What if we really believed people around us were so ready to receive, that if we opened up to them, we could lead them to

Christ? There could be a great harvest if we would just step out in faith and let God multiply our efforts. The harvest is plentiful and it is all around us. He is the Lord of the harvest (Matt. 9:37-38). He went before us and He is inviting us to join Him.

At this moment, when the disciples were challenged by Jesus, the hero of our story comes into the conversation. Andrew steps up and says, *"Here is a boy with five small barley loaves and two small fish."* Just to cover himself he adds, *"...but how far will they go among so many?"* This was the equivalent of a sack lunch, something like small muffins and dried sardines. What is remarkable is that it is a young boy who steps up in the middle of the crowd and says, "Here, you can take my lunch to Jesus for Him to use."

Undoubtedly, other people were there with food, maybe stuffed under their robe. But it was the boy that gave away his lunch. God loves to use ordinary people to accomplish extraordinary things, because He gets the glory. This boy wasn't used by God because he had the biggest or the best lunch, but because he gave his lunch to Jesus. This willingness to move from consumer to eager contributor was the little switch that took him from pauper to partner with God.

Isn't it amazing how such a small gift could spark such an incredible miracle? We see the eternal principle of sowing and reaping. God breaks through circumstances of lack with simple seeds of faith. What gets sown in God is multiplied forward and back. What you give always impacts others and causes you to receive more in return. This is not only true of the positive, but also the negative. As smiles and kindness are multiplied back to you, likewise are criticism and indifference.

While we are waiting for God to do something for us, God is waiting for us to sow seeds of faith, so He can do something through us. In any situation of need, God is waiting to activate His power and provision by our bold, powerful choices of love and faith that bring heaven to Earth. If only we could see the future in the seed that we all possess. There is a life full of miracles in that seed.

> *If only we could see the future in the seed that we all possess. There is a life full of miracles in that seed.*

There are powerful principles here. First, if there is something you are lacking, it is a sign that you need to sow seed. Not having enough in the areas of time, relationships, hope, kindness or help may be an indication you are not giving enough of those to God. Remember, it is always the seed you sow that determines the harvest you receive.

Second, giving God ownership of what you have increases its potential. It goes from enormous limitations to limitless possibilities. You may have heard this comparison: "A paint brush in my hand is a mess on the carpet, but in Leonardo

De Vinci's hand, it is a priceless masterpiece." A basketball in my hand is a brick against the board, but in LeBron James's hand, it is an NBA championship. A check and pen in my hand can pay the rent, but in Bill Gates's hand, it can start a billion-dollar corporation. It all depends on whose hand those things are in. When what little we have is in God's hands, all things are possible for us.

It is also important to note that it wasn't just what the little boy gave but *how* he gave it that released a miracle. He gave his lunch cheerfully, immediately, and willingly. You may have heard someone say, "God loves a cheerful giver, but He will take an offering from a grouch." That is funny but not really true. God doesn't need our money or anything else from us. If we can't give cheerfully, He doesn't want our gift, nor will it be something that He can multiply. God asks for our treasure for one reason: He wants our heart. He wants to transform us so that He can bless others through us. He wants us to have the joy and reward of partnering with Him in the miraculous, and see our needs met in the process.

It is critical to note that the boy gave his first fruits, his sole lunch, not some old leftovers. He also gave in faith, **expecting** God to do a miracle. What we give first is multiplied the most. So often our expectation determines our visitation. The Bible says the farmer sows in hope (I Cor. 9:10). We are to sow with praise, praying that God will do something amazing. It is the degree of our faith that determines the potential of our miracle.

In Luke 6:38 NIV, I love what Jesus said would happen when we give like this: *"Give, and it will be given to you. A good measure, pressed down, shaken together and running over, will be poured into your lap."* They used their robes as a kind of grocery cart. Imagine the picture of wheat or grain being poured into someone's apron until they can hardly stand up.

In the Old Testament, there are examples of miraculous provisions from God. One example is the bread from heaven (manna), that miraculously appears when the children of Israel wandered in the wilderness. It is interesting that God told them to gather only enough manna for their needs (Exod. 16). But as Jesus comes on the scene, He wants to reveal more of the plenty too much generosity of God. In this case, there were twelve baskets of food left over.

I wonder if Jesus sent the leftovers home with the little boy. If so, can you imagine what his mother must have thought: "Where did you get all of this?"

"Oh, I traded my sack lunch to Jesus for it."

"COOOOOOL! Do that again tomorrow!"

As great as the physical miracle was for the boy, no doubt the inner, spiritual miracle was far greater. We like to say that giving offerings is not God's way of raising funds, it's God's way of raising sons and daughters. Being prosperous

> *We like to say that giving offerings is not God's way of raising funds, it's God's way of raising sons and daughters.*

has nothing to do with a big bank account. It has to do with being a bigger and bigger channel of God's love, peace, hope, and joy to a desperate world. I believe from that day forward, this boy learned to live as a hose and not a sponge, as a river and not a reservoir. He learned that as you shovel out, God shovels in, and God has a far bigger shovel. I believe there was not only an incredible level of abundance on his life, but a new authority in his life.

Wayne Myers says that, as you are faithful to give out of God's storehouse, He then gives you the keys to it. Love and generosity move you into a place of authority to bring greater kingdom impact.

When I was 17-years-old, I loved camping and having cool camping gear. My dream was to own a duck-down sleeping bag. I was working at my first job and finally saved up enough money to buy it. I was so excited! That weekend we were doing outreach in downtown El Paso, where I met a homeless man and began witnessing to him. He told me that someone had stolen his sleeping bag and he didn't know what he was going to do. Well, you guessed it. Before I ever used it, I felt the Lord telling me to get my sleeping bag and give it to him.

Years later in reflecting back on that experience, I sense the Lord saying, "Dale, I want you to know that you will never lack a sleeping bag. But far more important, you will have a compassion and an authority to minister to the homeless and the poor that you haven't known before. You will bring My love and salvation to many of them in your lifetime." I can report that both of those things have been true.

My oldest son had a similar experience. We held a campaign to fund the purchase of a church building for our ministry. Jason had just recently graduated from college and was a new CPA. To my surprise, not only did he make a generous pledge to the building fund, he made an over-the-top, sacrificial pledge to give one-third of his income for three years as a seed offering for this project. I felt anxious for him, but he was at peace. During that time, God more than provided for his needs and he received many other blessings, including meeting his beautiful wife. But beyond all of that, he received authority in the areas of financial management.

Shortly after, God raised him up as the church treasurer and administrator. Like Joseph in the book of Genesis, he has had an amazing anointing and favor for managing not only his resources, but God's resources as well.

There is a story of a hiker who got lost in the desert and ran out of water. Miraculously, he came across an abandoned well house with an old-fashioned pump inside. He tried pumping but nothing came out. He did find a note on the well that said there was a jar of water buried a few feet away. He found the place and quickly dug up the jar. It had an interesting note on it saying, "Be careful, this jug contains just enough water to prime the pump. If you drink any of it, there won't be enough to get the well going. But once the well is primed and working, you will have more than enough to drink. P.S. And don't forget to fill the jar and bury it for the next traveler."

He was so thirsty, but he had to decide whether to settle for a drink or open a fountain. He made the right choice and when the well was primed, plenty too much water came out. When he buried the jar, he added to the note, *"DO IT! IT REALLY WORKS!"*

Some of you may be at that place in your life, living as a pauper with barely enough. God is waiting to open fountains from heaven. Dare to move by faith from getting to giving and watch what happens. Believe me, it really works!

APPLICATION

1. The purpose of a school test is to determine the level of our knowledge. Jesus has a higher purpose when He tests the disciples saying, *"You feed them."* What do you think was His purpose?

2. Impossible situations are opportunities for miracles. What humanly impossible situation does God want you to partner with Him for a miracle? What seed could you sow?

3. *Jesus has called us to be "fishers of men" but it is often easier to be keepers of the aquarium.* Can you answer the following?

    Who are my neighbors? (Names, marital status, children's names, interests, felt needs?) How would God have me be a good neighbor?

    What do I know about my community, city/nation? (Leaders, community strengths/problems?)How can I be a difference maker?

    *The harvest is all around us. The **Lord of the Harvest is inviting us to join Him.***

Chapter 9

SETTING THINGS IN ORDER/
THE MIRACLE IS IN THE
MANAGEMENT

"Jesus said, 'Have the people sit down.'"
"When they had all had enough to eat, He said to
His disciples, 'Gather the pieces that are left over.
Let nothing be wasted"   (John 6:10, 12 NIV).

What I love about this story of the loaves and fishes is that Jesus didn't just snap His fingers to bring food to people in need. He partnered with the disciples and the people in a way that helped them be good stewards and make the best possible use of the opportunity to receive and manage God's miracle.

God doesn't want mere consumers of His work, He wants partners. Miracles often don't look the way we imagine. We sometimes think of them in terms of magic, while God often intends to work them through management. For whomever received the leftover twelve baskets, it was no doubt a miracle of provision, but it was also a result of responsible follow through. This story is a perfect illustration of how God loves not only to work for us but through us. I believe that, by learning to be faithful with what God has put in our hands, we begin to experience God's fullness. We who are faithful in little become rulers over much (Matt. 25:23).

According to Colossians, Paul points to his success by saying, *"I also labor, striving according to His working which works in me mightily"* (Col. 1:29 NKJV). One key in moving from being a pauper to a partner with God is understanding that partnership is based on covenant integrity. We think of miracles as our ability to trust God, but they are equally dependent on whether He can trust us. Have you ever asked the question, "Can God trust me?"

> *Have you ever asked the question, "Can God trust me?"*

When it comes to money and material possessions, God's main concern is not how much we have but how responsibly we manage it. In the parable of the talents, we learn that how we manage earthly resources determines our ability to be trusted with eternal responsibilities. In Luke 16:11, Jesus asks, if God can't trust us with earthly wealth how will He trust us with "true riches" (spiritual blessing). God is preparing us for greater favor, opportunities, and responsibilities to reign with Him, not only here, but in heaven. The Bible says we're going to *"judge angels"* (I Cor. 6:3). I don't know what that means but I hope for the angels' sakes, we can get our act together down here.

I once heard the story of an evangelist who was on the road around Christmastime. He was trying to save enough money from offerings he received to provide his family with nice gifts. Just before Christmas, as he was ministering at a church, the Lord told him to give the money he had saved to a widow in need. He struggled a bit but obeyed. In a service that soon followed, a woman came in a wheelchair. She was obviously very near death. During the ministry time, the Lord gave him a word of knowledge and a gift of faith. When he prayed for her, she was miraculously healed. The Lord spoke to him and said, "Because you were faithful to help the poor widow, I was able to trust you with the anointing to heal the dying woman."

God is a good father and He loves to give good gifts to his kids. We know that every good and perfect gift comes from the Father of Lights (James 1:17). However, I believe there are times when God, in His goodness, withholds blessings and provisions from His children. He is not doing this to punish us. Instead, He knows that if He gives us a gift to steward that exceeds our maturity to manage it well, that gift could crush us. Luke 12:48 NKJV says, *"To whom much is given, to him much will be required."* We are so eager for the "much is given" part of the equation, but not always as committed to the "much is required" part. This is why growing in the revelation that we are called to be "kingdom managers" is so important.

Kingdom management is using the power and wisdom of God to take something small and grow it into something significant for God's kingdom. God has given each of us many unique gifts and talents and He also has given us the power to use those talents in such a way that opens the floodgates to *heavenly opportunities*.

> *Kingdom management is using the power and wisdom of God to take something small and grow it into something significant for God's kingdom.*

I believe there are four key practices of kingdom managers, when followed, bring a release of heavenly resources to our earthly realities. These include:

1. Becoming faithful stewards with "small beginnings"
2. Being relentlessly committed to personal (spiritual) growth
3. Becoming aware that they are managing God's assets (not their own)
4. Learning to receive and implement heaven's solutions for life's apparent lack.

By following these principles, we will transcend a life of scarcity and enter into the great bounty that God has in store for our lives.

Faithful stewardship is taking personal responsibility for doing your best wherever you're at with whatever you've got. Faithful stewards don't despise the day of small beginnings (Zech. 4:10). I'm convinced that one of their favorite verses is Job 8:7 NLT, *"Though you start with little you will end with much."* Faithful stewards don't look with jealously at the person with five talents, but instead ask themselves, "How can I be faithful with the one talent God has given me so He can trust me with more?" They refuse the mindset of a passive "wisher" that laments, "when I finally" or "if only I" (win the lottery/have more time/get caught up/ have more help...) "then I will do or be something great for God." Instead, they expect their miracle to happen through a process of faithful obedience. They are confident that: In the kingdom of God, if I plant just one seed, that seed can become a sprout, and that can become a tree, and someday, that tree will bear fruit and multiply until I have an orchard.

This reminds me of the story of Abraham, "The Father of the Faithful" (Rom. 4:16). Abraham was an ordinary man living in an ordinary tent, shepherding ordinary sheep, but carrying an extraordinary promise. God fulfilled His promise to Abraham and gave him a son and eventually, he multiplied Abraham's descendants to number more than the stars in the heavens. But it all started with one promise – one son.

Genesis 18:19 NLT reveals why the Lord decided to use Abraham in this way. He says, *"I have singled him out so that he will direct his sons and their families to keep the way of the Lord by doing what is right and just. Then I will do for Abraham all that I have promised."* In other words, as Abraham stewarded the "little" he had, *then* God did the *big* that He promised.

Secondly, kingdom managers are relentlessly committed to personal spiritual growth. Personal growth is not only doing the most with what I have, but becoming the most I can be through what God has given me. Someone once said, "Our potential is God's gift to us; what we do with it is our gift to God."

> *Personal growth is not only doing the most with what I have, but becoming the most I can be through what God has given me.*

We like to say, "Show me your glory" but God likes to say, "Let me grow my glory in you." Miracles increase on the outside the more we grow our faith on the inside. Luke 2:52 NIV says of Jesus as a child, *"He grew in wisdom and stature and in favor with God and man."* The miracles in Jesus's ministry didn't begin until he was 30 years old, but they were growing inside of Him as a little child.

After telling us about how the nature of God is connected with the promises of God, Peter says in 2 Peter 1:5-7 NIV, *"For this very reason, make every effort to add to your faith goodness; and to goodness knowledge; and to knowledge, self control; and to self control, perseverance; and to perseverance, godliness; and to godliness, mutual affection; and to mutual affection, love."*

In other words, growth happens as we draw from the Word the power, character and qualities of God so they can be applied to our lives. We grow when we not only receive the Word, but daily step out in simple acts of faith: each choice of faith activates more of the nature of Christ to be expressed through our lives.

Jim Whitaker, the first American to climb Mount Everest, said, "You can never conquer the mountain. You can only conquer yourself. You overcome sickness and everything else – your pains, aches, fears – to reach the summit."[17]

I remember once complaining to the Lord that I just wasn't good at administration. I was expecting a comforting word, like "I will send someone to help you," but what I received instead was a short and direct word from God: "Get good." God absolutely required growth from me. The tedious investment in learning about systems and planning prepared me to manage more of the assets and opportunities God later brought my way.

Thirdly, kingdom managers are profoundly aware that their role on Earth is to steward Christ's resources. They have made the switch from merely contributing to Christ's cause to effectively managing His assets. True stewards acknowledge the resources that are in their hands while freely handing over ownership of those resources to God. Psalms 24:1 NKJV makes it clear, *"The Earth is the Lord's and all its fullness, the world and those who dwell therein."* Many fall short of God's blessing because they don't move in alignment with this concept.

I heard Pastor David Swan share a story of taking his young son to McDonald's. He didn't order fries for himself, assuming that he'd just grab a few from his son. Much to his surprise, when he reached over to take some French fries, his son stopped him, "No Dad, they're MINE!" Rather quickly, a wide range of thoughts ran through Pastor Swan's mind including that his son wouldn't have been born if it wasn't for him, that he had bought the meal in the first place, and had the right to take the whole meal as his own... how dare he! Shortly after this, Pastor Swan had an "A-ha" moment of how God must feel when we do the same to Him.

God cannot pour out His full blessing onto us and onto our stuff until He has full possession. What He possesses, He blesses, and what we cling to as our own, He allows us to manage in our own strength. We often see this when it comes to finances. Personal finances are typically the famous "last stand" in surrendering to the Lord. I have found the greatest challenge for many people is understanding what it means to follow

> *What He possesses, He blesses, and what we cling to as our own, He allows us to manage in our own strength.*

Christ completely. We are fans willing to contribute to his work. But being complete followers, allowing Him to be in total control and have ownership of everything, is another story. Many people sort of choose Christ, hoping He will follow them and do what they want, rather than completely surrendering control to Him.

I heard an interesting story when one of the Northern European tribes turned to Christ in the Middle Ages. The "Franks" were warriors, so when they were baptized, they asked if they could keep the hand that held their sword above the water so they could keep killing with it.[18] In America, some might be tempted to ask if they could just keep their wallet out of the water.

It is important to realize that our assignment as partners with God depends on our alignment with God's authority. We don't defeat the enemy by shouting at the devil but by submitting to God. Paul tells the Corinthians he was willing to do spiritual warfare against some of the devastation that was coming against their lives. He said they could count on the enemy of their soul being punished *"once their obedience was complete"* (2 Cor. 10:6 NIV). In Malachi 3:10, the Lord told the Israelites He was ready to break the curse on their finances and rebuke the devourer once they had obeyed by bringing all the tithes into the storehouse.

I believe Scripture teaches that this transfer of ownership to God happens through a faith decision to give our first fruits to the Lord – what is called the "tithe" or tenth of our increase. This is not the lid for our giving, but a starting point, a stake in the ground designating who is the Owner of all of things.

In Romans 11:16 NIV, Paul establishes a principle that is repeated many times in Scripture: "*If the part of the dough offered as first fruits is holy, then the whole batch is holy; if the root is holy, so are the branches.*" In this case, when we tithe it sets apart the rest of our money to be under God's covering. I believe as we offer our tithe to the Lord we are entering a covenant partnership, allowing Him to sanctify and bless the other 90% as well. Malachi 3:10 is referred to as God's testing process. God invites us to tithe and test His faithfulness to provide. When we understand how faithful He is, we become more faithful and He can trust us with more.

D.L. Moody was once said to have met a man who expressed to him a rather distressing problem. The man bemoaned, "I used to tithe when I had less money, but now I'm making $5,000 a week. I can't imagine giving a tenth of that." In response, Mr. Moody laid hands on the man and prayed, "Dear Lord, please reduce this man's income to the level of his obedience."

I can testify how my life was impacted by clearly establishing God's ownership over my finances through tithing. As a newly married seminary student expecting our first child, I lost my job. We were living week to week and

I didn't have another job lined up. When I was figuring how to budget my last paycheck, it was tough to tithe, not knowing what lay ahead, but we did. That very Monday, I went to the park and was shooting a basketball, when a man drove up alongside the court and shouted, "Hey do you want a job?" I ended up getting a job making two dollars more an hour than I had previously earned, without ever missing a paycheck.

The most important thing this did was to establish a mindset assuring me that God was the owner of what I possessed and I would always be His partner. This would be huge when, not long after, I responded to God's call to plant our first church in Northeast El Paso. We felt led to move, though we had no job or congregation. Nevertheless, as we prepared to go, we had peace that God was the Owner and we were merely stewards of His enterprise.

As the time neared to make our big move, one financial miracle after another put God's great faithfulness on display and grew our faith big time. First, our old car was on the verge of collapsing. It burned a quart of oil every day. We used a hanger as an antenna. I went into the Ford dealership where an elder from our church worked, to see what kind of arrangement I could get for a car. Our friend asked me to start by pointing out the car I'd like to have. I pointed to a brand-new Ford Fairmont and said, "That one would be nice, but how would I pay for it?" He informed me that someone had anonymously come by and told him that they would pay for whatever car I picked out. I never found out who it was, but I have to confess the thought came to my mind, "Why didn't you pick a Mustang?"

A short time later, it was time for our daughter Heidi to be born and we didn't have insurance or the money for the hospital. As I went to the billing office before discharging, I jokingly asked, "If you don't have the money to pay the bill, does the hospital keep the baby?" After a bit of nervous laughter, the administrator excused herself for a moment, and returned with the news that we qualified for their special pastor's discount. "Is that even a thing?" I thought. Nonetheless, it was quite a significant amount. When I later called to thank them, they told me no such discount existed.

Well, I still owed them $600 and was praying about that. A couple of days later, someone ran into my bumper while I was parked at a stop sign. It all happened so fast. I remember the man offered to give me $750 on the spot for the damages. It was just a dent on my bumper so I agreed. That week, I took the car to a friend of a friend who fixed it for $100. I ended up with a car repair, $600 for the hospital, and enough left over for a celebration dinner with my family to welcome the new baby.

The fourth key to faithful management is learning to receive and implement innovative, creative ideas of wisdom that make room for God's blessing. I call it learning to dig the ditches for God to fill with rain. I remember the Lord challenging me to ask Him for the "Joseph anointing." God gave Joseph (a man who had been in prison) not only the revelation and wisdom to preserve Egypt and the world during a famine, but to do it in a way that brought great increase and long-term empowerment (Gen. 41). In Luke 16:8-9, Jesus credited the entrepreneurs of the world with being smarter in handling dishonest gain than the children of the kingdom. He comments, *"They are on constant alert, looking for angles, surviving by their wits. I want you to be smart in the same way – but for what is right – using every adversity to stimulate you to creative survival, to concentrate your attention on the bare essentials so you'll really live, really live, and not complacently just get by on good behavior"* (MSG). What an amazing thing to realize that we have the mind of Christ (I Cor.2:16).

This is illustrated so well in the story in 2 Kings 4:1-7 of a widow, whose husband had helped many of the prophets who refused to bow to Baal in Elijah's day. Tragically, her husband suddenly died, and left her in a desperate place. The creditors were about to close on her and force her sons into some kind of slavery. Instead of calling down money from heaven, Elisha challenged her to believe God would do a miracle through her management. She was to borrow as many empty vessels as she could from neighbors, to hold oil that she could sell. Perhaps, the neighbors weren't willing to give her oil, but they would give her empty vessels. In a powerful step of faith, she collected these vessels and began pouring oil into them out of her one partially full jar. Then the most amazing thing happened: the oil kept flowing until every vessel was filled. She was able to pay the debt and thrive. God wants to show us vessels in the form of methods, strategies and ideas He can use as platforms for resources and breakthroughs.

I love the fact that God is able to give us supernatural wisdom for helping the poor rise above poverty and thrive. Over the last 20 years, our ministry has helped hundreds of "hidden heroes" to grow their churches and ministries to become not only more self-sustaining but to contribute to the ministries of others. We have been able to help them develop projects and programs that facilitate not just receiving fish, as the saying goes, but teaching people to fish.

Many years ago, after ministering to a desperately poor tribe in the mountains of Mindanao in the Philippines, the Lord gave me a picture of aqueducts, or ditches, carrying water through the desert. We live in a desert area in New Mexico that was brought to life by a dam built nearly 100 years ago. It created a reservoir named Elephant Butte, through which the Rio Grande River flows and is managed. Through "water management" dry, desert places like Southern California and much of the Southwest have blossomed into fertile valleys, producing fruits and vegetables that feed our country.

It was from that vision I sensed and claimed a promise that God would provide both the strategies and means for developing and funding kingdom projects and programs through partners in many places around the world.

By the grace of God, we have seen well over 100,000 lives touched and impacted for Christ through building simple relationships and carving out strategies for God's love and compassion to flow.

APPLICATION

Four keys of kingdom management:
- Becoming a faithful steward with "small beginnings"
- Being relentlessly committed to personal (spiritual) growth
- Becoming aware you are managing God's assets (not your own)
- Learning to receive and implement heaven's solutions for life's apparent lack.

1. The smallest gesture can show a person that they are valued and appreciated. Can you describe a "day of small beginnings"?

2. Choose an area you would like to make a deeper commitment to grow personally/spiritually. Define what that means to you. Set reasonable goals. Journal your progress.

3. God has given you assets to help fill life's lack (spiritual gifts, abilities, personality, resources). In God's hands, even your most difficult experiences become assets. Share your spiritual story (three to five minutes) with a small group.

    What He possesses, He blesses...

Chapter 10

DISCOVERING ABUNDANCE BY PUTTING THE NEEDS AND INTERESTS OF OTHERS FIRST

He replied, "You give them something to eat"
(Luke 9:13 NIV).

Taking the five loaves and the two fish and looking up to heaven, He gave thanks and broke them. Then He gave them to the disciples to distribute to the people (Luke 9:16 NIV).

Whereas the call of God to the little boy was to give his lunch, the call of Jesus to the disciples was to give their time and strength to feed the crowd, as many as 15,000 people. So often the most valuable and costly acts of love involve not just our money, but our time and service. It's amazing to see how God not only can multiply loaves and fishes, but time and energy as we sow generously to His work.

In this story, we see a powerful principle of abundance. To the degree we follow God and put the interests, needs, and opportunities of others before ourselves, is the degree we see abundance flow. Our ability to put someone else in position to receive something they couldn't receive on their own automatically puts us in positions to receive and give even more.

In describing the "plenty too much mindset", Paul specifically challenges us in Philippians 2 to "*Let this mind be in you which was also in Christ Jesus...*" (verse 2:5 NKJV).

He further describes how Jesus, although comfortable in heaven, chose not to hold onto His rights, position or comfort but opted to relinquish the right to think of Himself. He laid all of his prerogatives as God aside in order to serve, by giving His life for us. Gerald Brooks, a friend of mine, was asked, "What is the key switch that makes you a Christian leader?" He replied, "Giving up the right to think of yourself." A plenty too much person recognizes this and continually seeks to add value to whoever they're with, wherever they are, all of the time.

This has been referred to as a "sower's mindset." I love the story of Johnny Appleseed, who, according to legend did something in the natural so simple yet profound. As he traveled west in the American frontier, he planted apple trees wherever he could so future travelers could be helped on their journey. He chose not just to go through life but to sow his way through life.

Jesus describes this as the definition of greatness. "If you want to be great," He said, "learn to be the servant of all" (Mk 9:35). He taught that if you want to be first in line in heaven, make a beeline to the end of whatever line you find yourself in here on Earth, and first help those ahead of you get what they need. He implied that, believe it or not, this is how you get to the front of the line. The switch in our thinking comes as we continually ask the question, "What is the opportunity to assist, build up and bring honor to people around me, in Jesus's name?" God's plenty too much resources flow through us when we think this way.

In fact, Jesus reduced all commandments of the Bible down to one: *"A new commandment I give you, that you love one another as I have loved you"* (John 13:34 NKJV). In other words, become a servant to all, the way He became a servant to you, and you will fulfill all of the commandments. Serving was the key that allowed the Father to lift Jesus up and give Him a name above every other name (Phil. 2:9-11).

Motivational speaker Zig Ziglar famously said, "You can get everything in life you want if you will just help enough other people get what they want."[19]

This way of thinking cuts against the grain of selfish thinking. It breaks the death grip that poverty has on the mind which says if others have more, I will have less; if they go higher, I go lower; if they are loved more, I will be loved less.

I had an interesting visit on an airplane with a man who had an important government position in the African nation of Senegal. In discussing the differences between richer nations and poorer ones like his, he shared what he tells his own people:

"In our country, we believe if someone is above us on the ladder, the only way for us to get further up is to throw off that person ahead of us. We have learned a "crab mentality" where, to be successful, we must pull down the success of others."

If only he could teach people the way of success is the exact opposite. If we will just focus on lifting people before us higher up the ladder, then we, too, will go higher.

If we will just focus on lifting people before us higher up the ladder, then we, too, will go higher.

James Keller said, "A candle loses nothing by lighting another candle."[20] Of course, lighting another candle makes the light twice as bright. I remember a Coke commercial where a growing line of people holding candles were singing, "I'd like to teach the world to sing in perfect harmony."[21] The lights kept multiplying and spreading as they sang. The scene impressed upon me that when God wants His abundance to flow, He builds bridges. Especially in the kingdom of God, our influence grows through relationships of unselfish serving and lifting up others. Mother Teresa said, "I can do things you cannot, you can do things I cannot; together we can do great things."[22]

For several years, Heart for the World Ministries had the privilege of hosting teenagers from around the country to serve on mission trips in Mexico. We called it "Extreme Mission". We trained and connected them with youth groups from Mexico to reach out and minister God's love to people in their community. This grew until hundreds of youth were involved, and thousands of lives in Mexico were touched by the transforming power of the gospel.

The word came to my heart, "What you are creating here is a snowball-effect." As I pondered what that meant, I realized the greatest impact our ministry will have for Christ won't come from just our ministry. We had been given the privilege to light candles that would light other candles that would eventually shine on hundreds of thousands of people we would never meet. The Lord gave my son Jason a word that we would touch a billion people through our ministry, multiplying the compassionate touch to places and generations we would never see.

En route to an evangelistic crusade in Zambia, Africa, I was praying for a special anointing to minister to remote tribes with a huge influence of witchcraft and resistance. I thought of Reinhard Bonnke, who in the past generation saw over 70 million people in Africa and other countries come to Christ through power evangelism, what he calls "evangelism with fire." There were many healings and signs and wonders accompanying the ministry. I prayed, "Lord, would you give me a Reinhard Bonnke anointing?" I felt the Lord tell me, "What if I did something better? What if I let you be part of blessing, training and imparting my anointing to thousands of Africans to whom I want to give a Reinhard Bonnke anointing?"

Interestingly, not long after I arrived in Zambia, my interpreter shared that, ever since he was young, he had dreamed of being an evangelist like Reinhard Bonnke. I had the privilege of spending time encouraging and imparting to him things the Lord had given to me.

Our ministry is dedicated to helping empower hidden heroes, like my interpreter, on the frontlines of poverty, to more effectively be the hands and feet of Jesus.

Jesus taught that unity and community are keys to abundance and increase, while division, isolation, and competition are root causes of poverty and decrease. Jesus prayed in John 17:21 NKJV, *"...that they all may be one, as You, Father, are in Me and I in You, that they also may be one in Us, that the world may believe that You sent me."* I found it interesting how people in Zambia view poverty and abundance.

I remarked that a certain person appeared to be very poor. Someone corrected me and said, "Oh no, they have a big family and many friends who care about them." I realized they actually saw poverty and prosperity in terms of relationships verses isolation.

Mother Teresa said the worst kind of poverty is loneliness.[23] If you're alone, your life and potential are diminished in every way, whereas in community, your protection and potential is increased in every way. As we look beyond the 'fruit' of poverty, we find its roots are isolation and division.

I heard a pastor say that a study in Orange County, California, found that at the root of poverty there was divorce and the breakdown of the family. Because marriages fell apart, kids were usually raised in homes without fathers, with a mom who is not only struggling to provide, but having fewer opportunities to complete her education and pass on a legacy of prosperity. As the Heritage Foundation reports: "Child poverty is an ongoing national concern, but few are aware that its principal cause is the absence of married fathers in the home. Marriage remains America's strongest anti-poverty weapon, yet it continues to decline."[24]

The heart of God's plan to break a spirit of poverty is in the community of Jesus Christ. When God's people connect in serving and loving each other, poverty is broken and potential explodes. This was the key in the early church that turned the world upside down. Even their enemies had to acknowledge that the secret of their irresistible, contagious power was in how they loved each other.

I love the Peanuts cartoon in which Lucy is watching a TV show and Linus wants to change the channel. He moves toward the remote control. Lucy intervenes by raising her hand.

> *The heart of God's plan to break a spirit of poverty is in the community of Jesus Christ.*

"You see these five fingers, Linus?" she says. "By themselves they are just fragile fingers. But when they come together," she continues, making a fist, "they make a lethal force that one dare not challenge."

As Linus walks back to his chair, he looks at his fingers and replies, "Guys, why can't you ever get it together?"[25]

This power of unity comes by putting others first. In addressing husbands and wives about marriage, I believe Peter says to honor each other in a way that doesn't first consider how to get the attention and honor you want, but rather seek to give the other person the honor and love they wish for in the marriage. He says to the wife, this will "win" over even someone who doesn't believe (1 Pet. 3:1).

This is how life, growth and love flourishes in a church. Once, when I was on a mission trip over Valentine's Day, my wife Sharon was feeling sad and neglected, even though she was in agreement with the mission. She wasn't sure how to handle her feelings, but then an idea came to her. She took note of all of the ladies in her women's group who might also be feeling lonely on Valentine's Day. She spent days figuring out gifts and flowers to secretly give to all of them. Later, she told me that it was one of the greatest Valentine's Days she ever had. She felt so much love and joy, even in my absence. I told her I was really happy for her but wasn't sure how I could afford all of her generosity. I decided to stay home on Valentine's Day the next year.

This same mindset helped Sharon grow a large and thriving ladies' ministry. On one occasion, she invited a young woman whom she was mentoring to lead the group. Instantly, Sharon recognized that this young lady was a gifted and talented teacher. She felt the Lord saying, "I have just blessed you with My favor. I have sent you someone who is anointed to reach even more people." Sharon could have felt threatened and jealous, but instead saw this sister as a gift. In celebration, Sharon helped her move up to become the main teacher, and the ladies' group rose to a new level. At the same time, people saw a greater anointing on Sharon as well, and she assumed leadership in other areas that made her more effective than ever.

When we can truly see their wins as our wins and their losses as our losses, it changes our perspective.

One of the most powerful expressions of an abundance mindset is the ability as Christians to look at other Christians in other churches and denominations from an abundance perspective. When we can truly see their wins as our wins and their losses as our losses, it changes our perspective, increases unity and God's ability to extend the boundaries of His kingdom through us. We are not "competitors" but "completers" of one another. Although we are many families, we are one family in Christ. The issue is not how many members are in our church but how many can be reached and discipled for Christ in our cities and the world, regardless of which particular church people attend. Jesus taught us that the more we think as one and act in unity, the more He is glorified, and the more people will come to believe in Him (John 17:21).

I have found that, although we sometimes struggle to weep with those who weep, we struggle even more to rejoice with those who rejoice. In many cities, the spirit of competition between pastors and churches grieves the Holy Spirit and stifles His work. When a church begins to focus on increasing numbers instead of rejoicing that the *kingdom of God* is growing, there is a tendency for jealousy and competition.

One of the most meaningful moments in my life came from a compliment given about my father by the pastor of a megachurch in the town where I grew up. Pastor Charles was used by God to raise up and lead a church of thousands of people. Rather than being celebrated by other pastors, he was instead heavily criticized and condemned. I ran into him one day not too long ago. He told me in the warmest way how grateful he was for my dad, Fred Walker. He said in those early days when he suffered so much criticism, my dad was the only pastor in the city who intentionally spent time encouraging him. Dad was so excited how God was using their church, despite the fact that several people in the church my dad pastored had left to go to this church. The end result was that both churches and ministries thrived.

Did my dad agree with every doctrine this other pastor was teaching? Not necessarily.

But he rejoiced that Christ was being preached and wanted to encourage that pastor.

Jack Hayford, pastor of First Foursquare Church in Van Nuys, California, had a similar experience. When the church was small, he engaged in intense prayer for revival. As he cried out passionately to the Lord one day, he felt his prayer had been answered. But then came the surprise caveat: "I will send revival to the Baptist church down the street." There was a short hesitancy, but Jack found grace to rejoice. Revival did come to the Baptist church. Perhaps because the Lord could trust Jack's heart, God sent revival to his church as well, and it flourished, becoming one of the largest and most influential ministries in the nation.[26]

Some might say, "Doesn't the Lord warn us to watch out for false prophets and test and expose false teaching?" Of course, we are to teach our people to test and discern the difference between true and false doctrine. We are to warn about those who, after repeated attempts to correct them of deliberately teaching error, are to be avoided. But I believe our spirit should be that of "agonizing" to keep the unity of the spirit in the bond of peace (Eph. 4:3), presuming innocence until, through a scriptural process, someone is publicly challenged or corrected. I believe the Lord's heart is especially broken by the vicious attacks that take place against ministers on social media. Beware, I say, of "sin sniffers" and "heresy hunters" who raise attacks out of a sectarian spirit rather than out of true love and discernment.

This abundance mindset is also critical when resolving conflict. Gerald Brooks adds a twist to one Bible verse and says, "Wherever there are two or three gathered together in His name, ...someone is going to get mad." Conflict is a normal and potentially healthy part of growing relationships, depending on how we view it. Relationships grow through a "good disagreement" handled in the way Jesus directed us, by humbly speaking the truth in love (Eph. 4:15).

In relationships, a poverty mindset too quickly concludes that we have "irreconcilable differences." An abundance mindset sees something and someone bigger than us. There is a God whose love is supernatural in us. I Corinthians 13:4-8 says love endures all things, it isn't easily provoked, it keeps no record of wrongs...it never fails!

We recently held a "Love After Marriage Conference" at our church. The host couple did an amazing job and transparently shared about how Jesus had healed and transformed their marriage. The wife shared, as part of the backstory, that their marriage had fallen apart when her husband confessed to having an affair. She was devastated. Preparing to leave and divorce him, she felt the Lord speak to her, "You can leave if you choose, but if you stay you can see Me give you the marriage you always dreamed of having." She stayed and through the application of God's divine love, their marriage was restored. Their testimony is now helping transform marriages around the world.

With a poverty mindset, we tend to react to conflict by drawing lines and acting threatened. We believe that for others to win a disagreement, we must lose and feel ashamed that we're wrong. In James 4:1-3 NLT, James talks about this: *"What is causing the quarrels and fights among you? Don't they come from the evil desires at war within you? You want what you don't have ... but you can't get it, so you fight and wage war to take it away from them. Yet you don't have what you want because you don't ask God for it. And even when you do, you don't get it because your motives are all wrong – you want only what gives you pleasure."*

An abundance person doesn't feel the need to win an argument to have what they want. They believe God cares for their interests and they put their desires in God's hands. They listen for, respect and desire God's greater good, even if it means losing an argument. I love the following poem by Edwin Markham.

> *He drew a circle that shut me out-*
> *Heretic, rebel, a thing to flout.*
> *But love and I had the wit to win:*
> *We drew a circle and took him in.*[27]

This applies to the most difficult of all choices: to forgive when we've been wronged. We all know how difficult it is when we've been betrayed, cheated or taken advantage of. We also know that we follow in the footsteps of the greatest Forgiver of all time. Even as Jesus faced the worst indignity and cruelty humans could inflict, the Bible says that it was *"for the joy set before Him, He endured the cross"* (Heb. 12:2 NKJV). Jesus, in His love, saw us, He saw the Father's plan, even in betrayal.

> *We follow in the footsteps of the greatest Forgiver of all time.*

When Peter drew his sword to defend Jesus from the soldiers, Jesus said, *"Put your sword away! Shall I not drink the cup the Father has given me?"* (John 18:11 NIV). Jesus saw through the suffering and recognized God's purpose to save us. He saw God's power to overrule and redeem man's cruelty.

Joseph, in a similar way, forgave his brother who betrayed him by this abundance perspective. He said to them, *"You meant it for evil against me; but God meant it for good, in order to bring it about as it is this day, to save many people alive"* (Gen. 50:20 NKJV). It is our faith in the Sovereign goodness and power of God that lifts us above the wrongs of others and frees us from the bondage of a victim mentality regardless of what we've gone through. Psalms 76:10, in The Passion Translation says, *"You have power to transform man's futile anger into praise. The fury of your enemies only causes your fame to increase."* This faith in God's power can move us from being held captive to hurtful circumstances to becoming confident in what He is about to do for us.

This perspective allows us to take one of the most important steps of faith: to *"put on love"* (Col 3:14 NIV). The Bible doesn't say try to work up love, or try to feel love; it just says, "Put on love." This is where people living out of their own sufficiency can never succeed. I saw a bumper sticker that said, "God loves you and I'm trying." Nothing about that warmed my heart. We all know how lame it feels when someone is "trying" to love you. But Christians are confident that Supreme love lives inside of us because Jesus lives in us. We may not feel it, sense it, or even be assured we want it, but it is what flows in us through the Holy Spirit (Rom. 5:5).

How do you put on love? The same way the disciples saw loaves and fish multiply. It is by a bold act of faith, believing that in stepping out, the supernatural love of God will flow through you.

Corrie Ten Boom was a young woman when the Nazis invaded her native Holland. Her family hid Jews from the Nazis and were eventually discovered. Her father and sister died in the concentration camps and Corrie suffered tremendously. After the war, she became a minister who freely shared her testimony in many places. She told the story of a Nazi prison guard who came up to her after one of her talks. When she recognized him, she froze. Hurt, anger, horror – the worst feelings arose in her. He was responsible in part for her sister's death and other atrocities. Holding out his hand, he told her he had become a Christian and was asking for her forgiveness. A battle waged in her mind. She told the Lord she could never forgive, and she needed to just turn and walk away, but the Lord revealed to her that He was there. He had all that she didn't have for this situation, and she was to take a step of faith. She managed to reach out her hand. It was like volts of electricity shot through not only her hand but her whole being. As she spoke forgiveness, a river of compassion and healing grace flowed through her. Not only was she able to forgive, her heart became healed at the most profound level.[28]

No matter what we've been through or what we face, the grace and power of God's love is great enough to heal our pain.

No matter what we've been through or what we face, the grace and power of God's love is great enough to heal our pain.

This doesn't always mean that it is safe to develop a deep, ongoing relationship with someone who has wronged you. It *does* mean we can always overcome the weight of bitterness and hurt in any relationship. Where might God want to multiply love or forgiveness that you don't feel in your heart right now?

APPLICATION

When God's people connect in serving and loving each other, spiritual poverty is broken and potential explodes.

1. Can you describe when: Someone encouraged you at a time you needed it most? You were an outsider and someone drew you in? Someone joyfully celebrated your win?

2. Where might God want to multiply love or forgiveness that you don't feel in your heart right now?

3. Someone said that we are either a minus, a zero, or a plus in the life of everyone we interact. Can you think of an example of God giving you the opportunity to be a plus in someone's life this week?

What is the opportunity to assist, build up and bring honor to people around me, in Jesus's name?

Chapter 11

TAPPING INTO THE ABUNDANCE OF GOD THROUGH PRAYER

*"And He directed the people to sit down on the grass.
Taking the five loaves and the two fish and looking
up to heaven, He gave thanks and broke the loaves"*
(Matt. 14:19 NIV)

We would be remiss to consider how to tap into the abundance of God for the needs of Earth, without acknowledging the crucial role of prayer. Preceding the multiplication miracle, Jesus lifted His eyes in prayer and gave thanks. Jack Hayford said, "Prayer is invading the impossible."[29]

This was the case here. Jesus showed us how God uses prayer as a portal by which Heaven touches Earth. This wasn't just any kind of prayer, but what the Bible refers to as "the prayer of faith." For example, James says it is the prayer of faith that brings healing to the sick (James 5:15).

Jesus's prayers weren't so much about bombarding Heaven with requests, but about partnering with the Father to see that His works and His will are done on Earth as in heaven (Matt. 6:10). Jesus viewed the needs of Earth differently. We already mentioned the passage in Isaiah 65:24 NIV, where the Lord says, *"Before you call, I will answer."* Jesus did not see heaven waiting around for our sincerity or our requests to respond to Earth. Initiative and power are released from heaven in order for us to recognize and respond to it. Jesus explained that, *"The Son can do nothing by Himself; He can do only what He sees His Father doing, because whatever the Father does, the Son also does"* (John 5:19 NIV).

When Jesus prays at Lazarus' tomb, even though Lazarus has been dead for four days, Jesus doesn't struggle to believe. He calmly affirms, *"Father, I thank you that you have heard Me. I knew that you always hear Me..."* (John 11:41-42 NIV). When He hears that Lazarus has died, He has such a different reaction than we would have. He says, *"...I'm glad I wasn't there, because now you have another opportunity to see who I am so that you will learn to trust in Me"* (John 11:15 TPT). Jesus didn't see Himself as a beggar requesting something from the Father, but as an ambassador having faith in the Father who wanted to bring provision in this situation.

This approach to prayer has become our right and privilege through Christ. When Jesus gave us His name to use in prayer, it was as if He were giving us checks signed with

His signature to draw from the storehouse of the Father as the Holy Spirit would direct.

According to *Helps Word-studies*, the meaning behind the Greek word 'ónoma' (name) means "the revelation of someone's character that distinguishes them from all others. Thus, praying in the name of Christ means to pray as directed and authorized by Him, bringing revelation that flows from being in His presence. Praying in Jesus's name is not just a religious formula".[30] It is, by the Holy Spirit, expressing prayers that we are as assured of being answered as if Jesus Himself were asking.

In Christ, we are emissaries of a King bearing His authority. His name is a scepter or badge we have the right to use, much like the rod Moses used to part the Red Sea. Many Christians never come into this boldness in prayer because they haven't fully grasped and appropriated their righteousness in Jesus. They feel unworthy, and it is demonstrated in the way they pray – more as a slave than a son or daughter on a mission from the King.

I heard a story of a wealthy businessman who ran into a homeless man begging on the streets. He recognized him from high school and wanted to help him get back on his feet. So, he wrote a sizable check and gave it to him. A few weeks later, he found the man in the same place begging. He asked, "What happened?"

"I didn't have any clean clothes and I'm so dirty and smelly, I didn't believe the bank would cash the check, so I just left it in my pocket," the beggar replied.

Frustrated, the businessman said, "My friend, don't you know? They don't cash the check based on how you look or who you are. They will cash it because my signature is on it."

It is the same with us. When we stand in Jesus's righteousness, we have confidence that all the promises of God are ours in Christ Jesus because of what He did, not because of who we are (2 Cor. 1:20).

> *When we stand in Jesus's righteousness, we have confidence that all the promises of God are ours in Christ Jesus because of what He did.*

The story of the multiplication miracle reveals important elements that we can observe about praying in faith. I'd like to summarize them with the words:

- Preparation
- Exaltation
- Clarification
- Declaration

Before Jesus even prayed the prayer, He had already directed the people to sit down and prepare for the miracle. When it comes to an abundance mindset, facing everything in life from a perspective of faith is absolutely key.

In Mark 9:23 NKJV, Jesus says, *"All things are possible to him that believes."* He was challenging a father to be part of the miracle his son needed, by engaging his heart in faith. The man pleaded, "Lord, if you can do something, heal my son." Jesus said, in essence, "No, if you can believe in Me and bring your faith to this situation for Me to work through, your son will be healed."

We are commanded over and over to believe. The day after the crowd experienced the miracle feeding, they came to Jesus asking, *"What must we do to do the works God requires?" Jesus answered, "The work of God is this: to believe in the One He has sent"* (John 6:28-29 NIV).

This is a remarkable and important concept for us to grasp. God doesn't actually decide the level of blessing He will bring on our lives, *we* decide the level of God's blessing we will receive. God doesn't bless according to the level of our need but according to our **faith**. There are many people with needs and no blessing.

Rick Warren, author of the *Purpose Driven Life*, who has been an incredible influence around the world, was asked why he thought God had used him and Saddleback Church so immensely. His answer intrigued me. He said it is certainly not because he was better, smarter, or holier than others. He explained, "I believed God has blessed us so much simply because we have always expected Him to. In everything we've tried, we have expected that God would exceed all of our expectations and do beyond what we could ask or think."

One of his quotes, which I have kept on my wall, demonstrates the expectation he has in prayer for volunteers, and gives us a key to understanding how his ministry has raised up thousands of volunteers. He prays:

> "I thank you, Lord, that great people are ready to help me in the right time, in the right way, people I don't even know yet. I promise I'll never give up because I don't have the help, but I will trust God to provide. I agree to commit my way to the Lord. I trust Him to help me do it and He will. I believe God has the resources to help me that I have not even considered yet. There are multiplied thousands of persons with all sorts of talents, skills, concerns, and contacts that God will bring into our lives to fulfill His plans. So, I open my eyes and see the faces of people that will come towards me. I open my ears to hear what they're saying. Today, tomorrow, next week, I'll meet someone who is just the person I need, knowing that God has arranged it so beautifully."

During the early part of the last century, Norman Grubb (another spiritual hero of mine) was a missionary who, after founder C.T. Studd's death, assumed the leadership of Heart of African Mission Organization, now known as Worldwide Evangelization Crusade.[31]

As leader of the organization, he explained that God gave them the faith to believe for people and resources to send into missions. They prayed for such resources with this assumption:

> "How could we be such fools as to limit our plans for world evangelization to our visible and immediate bank balance, when the treasury of heaven is ours? To do this would be to walk in the flesh and not in the Spirit."[32]

How many fall short by posturing in prayer but not really believing and acting in faith? I heard about a preacher who called the townspeople to come to the city park for a special time of prayer to end the devastating drought that had plagued their county. As they gathered, he challenged them, "How many of you really believe God can send the rain?" Everyone shouted in agreement that they believed in miracles. He responded, "Well then, I have another question for you. Why didn't you bring your umbrellas?"

My dad taught me about faith when I was just a young boy, and there was one incident where it especially came in handy. Dad informed us that he was leaving El Paso on a business trip to California the next day. Of course, I thought of Disneyland and the beach, and asked if I could go. He said, "I don't think so, you've got school and chores." I was disappointed as I lay in bed. I don't remember where I heard it, but somehow, I had learned that "You should expect a miracle." So, I secretly packed a suitcase, rose very early, and was waiting at the car as he was preparing to leave. It must've impressed him because he said something like, "According to your faith, may it be done to you." I got to go with him to California.

I believe the Bible teaches if you are going to err, err on the side of being too audacious in your prayers. Always assume the greatest, most amazing thing you could imagine happening is a simple thing for the Lord. When I was leading my first Bible study as a high school student, we had lots of people coming to Jesus in our lunch-time session, but because there were two lunch shifts, people in the other shift couldn't participate. As I brought up the suggestion that we should pray, a young Christian stood and prayed boldly for a miracle that the school would decide to have just one lunch shift. Honestly, that stretched me, and I admit that I was thinking, "I hope this new Christian doesn't feel too disappointed if this doesn't happen." Within one week, over the intercom came the announcement that the school was going to one lunch shift. I was shocked and told myself, "Next time, don't be the guy with shrinking faith." The beautiful thing is, as a result of one young man's prayer of faith, our Bible study ministry exploded in growth and there was a great revival.

Another element of the prayer of faith is **exaltation**. Jesus lifted His eyes to heaven and gave thanks. One of the primary factors that determines our level of faith, and our ability to hear from God and know His will, is an accurate view of His greatness. A.W. Tozer noted: "What comes into our minds when we think about God is the most important thing about us."[33] If you have a big God, you have small problems, but if you have a small God, you will always have big problems.

Bill Bright was unquestionably one of the greatest men of faith of the last century, whose impact of faith included founding Campus Crusade for Christ and developing the Jesus Film Project. When asked the key to growing in faith, he said, "The most important thing you could do to grow your faith is to study and immerse yourself in the reality of the attributes of God." Faith grows when we realize how big, how good, and how able God is.

> *Faith grows when we realize how big, how good, and how able God is.*

Here is that switching point again. We switch from a scarcity to an abundance mindset as we worship, give thanks, and grow in our awareness of how great He is as we pray.

When we do this, we automatically dream bigger, pray bigger, and attempt bigger challenges for the Lord.

I remember a cartoon that featured two Eskimo ice fishermen going for a catch on a frozen lake. It wasn't hard to tell which one had the abundance mindset and which had the poverty mindset. The man with the poverty mindset carved out a hole in the ice as wide as a manhole cover. The other dug one the size of a whale! Can you see the difference? In the end, no matter how big a fish might be willing to bite the bait, the first man was only going to catch a fish that could fit through the size of a manhole cover.

In many ways, I believe our faith is like a mirror, a reflection of the God we see in our spirit. As we worship and walk in accordance with who He is, we shrink our doubts and grow in our capacity to sense, see, and hear what God has for us. I like the story of the boy whose friend noticed him staring at the bully next door through the wrong end of a telescope, with the lens that makes the image appear farther away.

"Why is your scope turned around?" he asked.

"Oh" he said, "the bully looks a lot smaller through this end."

That is a good example of looking through the lens of our natural perspective, versus learning to faithfully look at life through the lens of God's perspective. David looked at a giant in this way and saw him like an ant, compared to his God.

Focusing on God's greatness allows us to transcend the "facts" of a situation to God's perspective. God never calls us to ignore the facts. He does call us to see that His truth is much bigger than just the facts. In his book, *Experiencing God*, Henry Blackaby said, "You never know the full truth about a situation until you've heard from Jesus."[34] I love that because it drives us to not merely react to life, but to listen to Jesus and expect Him to intervene in our lives.

While the storm raged, Jesus was sleeping, because He already knew His Father would take care of it and they were going to the other side (Matt. 8:23-27). This was similar to the occasion when the woman caught in the act of adultery was thrown at His feet and He started writing in the sand (John 8:1-11). It is easy to look at the natural facts about difficult situations we face. But God wants us to sense that He has another word and plan, and to pray that truth into our situations.

> *The goal of prayer is not to bring our ideas to God, but to discern His will so we can pray authoritatively to change the world.*

This perspective prepares us for the next aspect of the prayer of faith: **clarification**. The goal of prayer is not to bring our ideas to God, but to discern His will so we can pray authoritatively to change the world.

Jesus already knew what He was going to do with the loaves and fishes. I believe in lifting His eyes giving thanks, He was showing us how, in times of need, we should lift our hearts to discern what God has for us. Identifying His voice in the situation we're in is so crucial. I like to imagine myself as the centurion who told Jesus *"... just say the word, and my servant will be healed"* (Matt. 8:8 NIV). When we understand that all we need is a word of confirmation from God for what He wants done, we have the keys to open the storehouse of heaven for our needs on Earth.

Acts 13 models doing this as a ministry team. As ministry leaders, our primary job is to allow the Holy Spirit to be in charge by discerning and activating God's will together through prayer. Acts 13:2 NKJV says, *"As they ministered to the Lord and fasted, the Holy Spirit said, 'Now separate to Me, Barnabas and Saul for the work to which I have called them'".* In sensing the Lord's direction for sending out Paul and Barnabas, they changed the world. This story illustrates the importance of taking the time in critical areas to wait on the Lord, seeking to discern God's will. This may include worship and fasting; it could also include discussions, investigation of scripture, perhaps the evaluation of prophetic words. The key is that we discern and come into agreement with what God wants us to ask of Him. When we do this, we can then in faith pray a prayer that releases the advancement of God's

> *The question is never whether God is speaking, the question is always: Are we listening?*

115

kingdom on Earth. In 1 John 5:14-15, John tells us if we ask anything according to His will, we know that we will have the petition we have asked for.

I believe God loves to speak to His children. The question is never whether God is speaking, the question is always: Are we listening and recognizing what He wants to show us? In Jeremiah 33:3 NIV, the Lord told Jeremiah, *"Call to Me and I will answer you and tell you great and unsearchable things you do not know."*

This leads us to step four: the declaration of faith, or **speaking** the word of faith. In Mark 11:22-23 NKJV, Jesus said, *"...Have faith in God. ...whoever says to this mountain, 'Be removed and be cast into the sea,' and does not doubt in his heart, but believes that those things he says will be done, he will have whatever he says."* In the case of feeding of the multitudes, the word of faith was, "Give them something to eat."

There comes a point in prayer where the Holy Spirit gives you a witness. It is a time to believe that what you have been asking for is already done. Though you can't prove it, you know God has given you confirmation that this is His will and you speak it as done. Certainly, there are mysteries and there are no formulas. I have my share of petitions that I am still waiting to see granted. But I have also found that God honors in amazing ways this partnership, in which we boldly declare the word of faith.

One such example took place in our journey to acquire property to build a facility for Heart for the World Church. As a church plant, it took close to three years to save $10,000 towards the purchase of property. During prayer, the Lord first spoke to one of our church elders, then confirmed to the rest of us, that we were to give this money away as a seed. We gave the entire amount to a missionary who was doing a great work. It was amazing how the Lord used that test of faith to begin opening the windows of Heaven and sparking expectation that something remarkable would take place.

Over the next several months, God began to move, and we were able to purchase fourteen acres of land at a very good price. We thought this was really it. For the next three years, we saved and drew up plans to build a 12,000-square-foot building on the property. Though we were excited and ready to go, we ran into one roadblock after another. The most difficult came when we needed a permit to widen the road in order to access our land, and the property owners next to us fought this. We began feeling we were at a dead end.

Just then, I received an unexpected call from a large church seeking to relocate and build on the other side of town. The pastor was a friend of mine and asked if we'd be interested in looking at their building. It was very impressive. It was over 35,000 square feet, and it had two kitchens and two sanctuaries. It was accommodating enough to double our present congregation. But, of course, the price was much more than we had planned to pay. It all seemed plenty too much. I was getting ready to tell the pastor we loved it but couldn't afford it when my wife challenged me with a good "Where is your faith" talk.

As elders, we decided to have a time of prayer and called the church to also pray. During those moments, the Holy Spirit kept confirming that this was our building. Finally, we declared the word of faith. We not only spoke it in our prayer meeting but also before the whole church, announcing that we believed it was done, that God had given us our property and we were excited to see how it would happen. To purchase it would require a $500,000 down payment, due in just a few months, of which we had less than $100,000. However, the very next week without having proceeded yet, I received a phone call. The person on the other end was interested in purchasing our land. They asked what price we'd consider in selling.

Remarkably, we hadn't put it on the market, advertised, or even mentioned that we wanted to sell it. Almost without thinking I said, "$500,000 cash" – almost twice what we had paid for it. To my shock, the man said, "We'll take it" and had a check for us by the end of the week. By the time we made the down-payment on our new building, we realized that the $10,000 seed had grown by God's grace to over $700,000.

In each subsequent step towards the building purchase, at times it appeared we would face lack, but we always ended up having more than enough. As great as acquiring the building was, the far greater miracle was the growth in our congregation's faith, expressed both in the prayers of faith and the act of faith in sowing that $10,000 seed. If we would listen and join Him in boldly praying His prayers, literally nothing would be impossible for us!

APPLICATION

The story of the multiplication miracle reveals important elements about praying in faith.

Preparation: Believing and getting ready for answered prayer
Exaltation: Worshiping, thanking God, celebrating His greatness
Clarification: Lifting our hearts to God to discern what He has for us
Declaration: Speaking a word of faith

1. How did Jesus demonstrate the above in such a way that the disciples not only witnessed a miracle but became partners in the miracle?

2. Jesus gave us the privilege of using His name in prayer. Describe what the name of Jesus means to you.

3. What are some ways that have helped you discern what God has for you?

4. Jesus saw what the Father was doing and boldly spoke the "word of faith". He said: "You feed them"- to the disciples, "Be clean"- to the leper, "Get up"- to the paralytic.

There are times when God has given us confirmation of His will and we speak it as done. What do you see the Father doing? Is it time to ask or speak a word of faith?

If we would listen and join Him in boldly praying His prayers nothing would be impossible for us!

Chapter 12

RELEASING GOD'S ABUNDANCE THROUGH SERVICE OF ORDINARY PEOPLE

"Then, breaking the loaves into pieces, He gave the bread to the disciples, who distributed it to the people. They all ate as much as they wanted, and afterward, the disciples picked up twelve baskets of leftovers" (Matt. 14:19b-20 NLT).

The significance of feeding the 5,000 was that it was among the first of Jesus's miracles in which His disciples were not just spectators but participants. Jesus could have made bread fall from heaven like He did in the Old Testament, but this time, He had a different plan. He wanted to work the miracle through the hands of the disciples.

One of the most important ways Jesus brings the resources of Heaven to meet the needs of Earth is by using ordinary people to do extraordinary things. I love that Jesus put this miracle in the hands of these disciples, who moments earlier

> *Jesus brings the resources of Heaven to meet the needs of Earth by using ordinary people to do extraordinary things.*

didn't even believe it was possible for Him to feed this many people with so few loaves and fish.

Surprisingly, God chooses weak, flawed, sometimes "goofy" people like us to bring His kingdom. Why not just do it Himself? Why not at least use angels? Yet in Ephesians it says that according to His eternal purpose, God has decided to make known His spectacular wisdom to the rulers and authorities in the heavenly realms through us, His church (Eph. 3:10-11).

According to John Wimber, founding leader of Vineyard Churches, God has determined that every Christian should get to do the ministry of Jesus (the most important thing on this planet). Wimber would say, "Everyone gets to play."[35]

God is preparing to pour His spirit out on all of us (educated, uneducated, men, women, teenagers, little kids, grandmas, old bald guys, guys with lots of hair, intellectuals, laborers, nerds, athletes) so that we can all prophesy, see visions, and be "the hands and feet of Jesus." Jesus has promised to take the gifts of heaven and "put the cookies on the lowest shelf" so everybody can give away His words, works, and wonders (Acts 2:17-18).

Remarkably, Jesus said to his disciples in John 14:12-13 NIV, *"Very truly I tell you, whoever **believes** in me will do the works I have been doing, and they will do even greater things than these, because I am going to the Father. And I will do whatever you ask in my name..."*

I believe Jesus taught us that a "normal" Christian is someone who, by the power of the Holy Spirit, attempts to do what Jesus would do for people, (feed and heal people, show kindness, share the gospel...) wherever they are. For this to happen, a scarcity mindset must be broken. Satan is terrified of the ministry of Jesus. If he can't stop it completely, he will devise every scheme possible to limit our vision about where ministry can happen, and who it can happen through.

One attitude that has plagued the church is a "fortress mindset." Many people, when they read the Lord's promise in Matthew 16:18 that the gates of hell shall not prevail against the church, picture the enemy surrounding our circled wagons. The opposite is true. Jesus is saying the church is on the offense and the devil's kingdom is surrounded as we charge with our battering ram. Demons realize they can't stop the invasion of the church from breaking in to rescue the lost, desperate and broken from Satan's captivity. The bars of hell are like spaghetti to the advance of the warriors of the Gospel.

I am convinced that one of the most important shifts in coming into an abundance mindset is realizing our capacity to be used by God.

At a Willow Creek Leadership Summit, I heard Craig Groeschel share an interesting experience at a swimming pool. A CEO coach approached him with a challenge: "I bet you can't hold your breath under water for a full minute."

Craig accepted the challenge. As he went under, he could hear coach telling him how many seconds had lapsed. After what seemed an eternity, he began to visualize Jesus in heaven; he heard "sixty seconds" and swung up out of the water. Coach told him "Not bad for a beginner. But I guarantee next time you can do it twice as long."

After teaching him some breathing techniques and learning to trick his brain into thinking he was about to take a breath, Craig was shocked to discover that on his second try, he could stay under water two minutes and forty-five seconds. Coach explained, "Your body is capable of doing more than your mind believes is possible."[36]

When it comes to our capacity to be used by the Lord, so many of us have a poverty mindset. We look at our flaws, weaknesses, and mistakes. We so easily respond to God's call by telling the Lord, "Here I am, but don't send me! You should send him or her." But God wants to show us He has given us a capacity in Him so much greater than we have ever thought or imagined.

> *God has given us a capacity in Him so much greater than we have ever thought or imagined.*

Even as it relates to our families and our children, God wants to help us switch from a "fortress mentality" to a "force mentality." It is easy to let fear control how we think as parents. In a world with so many bad influences, it is understandable that we want to protect and shield our families as much as possible.

At the same time, God wants us to teach our children to be bold and confident in standing up for the light. They can be taught the confidence and boldness to be the ones who influence their friends toward Jesus and away from the world's values (not the other way around). Our young people can see themselves as a far greater threat to the devil and his kingdom than he is to them. Greater is He that is in us than he that is in the world *(*I John 4:4).

During Extreme Mission (mentioned in Chapter 10), we challenged youth to believe they were being sent just as Jesus sent the disciples on their first mission trip, when He charged them, *"As you go, proclaim this message: 'The kingdom of heaven has come near'. Heal the sick, raise the dead, cleanse those who have leprosy, drive out demons. Freely you have received, freely give"* (Matt. 10:7-8 NIV).

I will never forget how God used these teenagers. They showed up chewing gum with earphones in their ears, holes in their jeans, playing video games on their electronic gadgets. Typical teens, none of them claiming any big spiritual résumés, they just prayed "Jesus use me." I remember these kids bringing the gospel to an indigenous group of Pima Indians in central Mexico and seeing an entire village come to Christ. One group brought a young deaf girl to the meeting. These young teenagers gathered around her and as they prayed, suddenly her ears were opened and she received her hearing. I saw what I believe is the new normal God wants every Christian to walk in. God wants His ordinary people in their ordinary strength to give what they have in their own ordinary way, so that He can use them to do *extraordinary* things that will change the nations of the world.

Martin Luther reintroduced the doctrine of the "priesthood of all believers" during The Reformation. He thought the word "priest" should become as common as the word "Christian" because all Christians are priests.[37] But to this day, many laymen or non-paid church members still carry a second-class mentality. They think of the clergy as having a special track with God, making them chief participators, while the main role of the church member is that of spectator: to pray, stay, and get out of the way.

But Jesus emphatically sent the Holy Spirit to break that mindset. The Holy Spirit has come to turn the entire church from an audience to an army. The world will be most effectively reached by the ***whole*** church taking the ***whole*** gospel to the ***whole*** world.

> *The world will be most effectively reached by the **whole** church taking the **whole** gospel to the **whole** world.*

This scarcity mindset began to switch in me as a naïve, unqualified 16-year-old. There was a revival called the *Jesus Movement* taking place in our town. I was excited about inviting friends to a Friday night youth service called "Jesus Chapel." As far as I know, everyone I invited got saved. After one service, I took a friend up to one of the leaders, Josh Villaseñor. He was only 19-years-old, but I saw him as the "reverend" because he was preaching at the service. I asked if he would help my friend meet Jesus and be filled with the Holy Spirit.

"No," he told me. I was stunned.

"What do you mean?" I said.

He basically told me that the same Holy Spirit who was in him was in me and that God would use me. I was sort of a nervous wreck. I thought, "What if I mess up this friend's eternal salvation and he never comes back?" To my amazement, with my feeble explanation of the gospel and uninspiring prayer, the guy not only was saved but, as I lay hands on him, was filled with the Holy Spirit. I remember looking at my hands afterward thinking, "Never thought these hands could do that."

This experience boosted me to gather a few kids in my high school and share the idea that we should start a Bible study. We weren't sure who should be the leader, but because I had been serving God for almost a whole month, they decided it should be me. (I guess that is how I got called to the ministry.) Although there could not have been more unqualified people, who shared some of the worst theology in our sermons, God used us. Our Bible study grew to more than 100. Many were saved and several eventually became full-time pastors and missionaries.

Another way the scarcity mindset has affected the church is our expectation of the average Christian in terms of ministry potential. I was raised in a church tradition which taught that healing the sick, casting out demons, speaking in tongues, having prophetic visions, angelic visitations, or words of knowledge ended after the age of the apostles. As I began to be exposed to the Charismatic and Pentecostal movements, I realized this wasn't the case, but I also developed the opinion that only "anointed men of faith and power" could see that happen. If we wanted to experience signs and wonders, we would probably have to go to a meeting held by someone like Oral Roberts, Kathryn Kuhlman, or Benny Hinn.

What changed my entire view was a visit to John Wimber's Vineyard Church in the 1980s. I saw teenagers and all kinds of ordinary people, not only in the church but on the streets, praying for the sick and seeing God do miracles. Wimber shared his conviction and experience that the "Good news then, is still the Good news now. *"Jesus Christ is the same yesterday, today, and forever"*. (Heb. 13:8 NLT) Today, these same signs, such as laying hands on the sick and seeing them healed, will follow those who believe (Mark 16:17-18). Although Wimber was also from a conservative evangelical church background, he began to realize the Bible taught that we would "do the stuff" Jesus did. He began to pray for the sick simply out of obedience to God's Word.

The significant shifts in my thinking about the supernatural came as I discovered God's power doesn't flow through us because of our anointing or ability, but because of our simple obedience. The Holy Spirit gifts aren't something we perform on our own. They come about through our partnering with Him in what He is already doing all around us, all the time. The disciples participating in feeding the multitudes is a good example.

There is no suggestion that the disciples felt a special anointing. They didn't have a rushing feeling going through them, they weren't shaking and acting like some powerful evangelist on spiritual steroids. In a very natural way, Jesus handed them the bread and as they obeyed, the miracle happened. I personally think they may have been "sweating bullets."

In my imagination, I see myself in one of the disciples' shoes. I've never seen a miracle like this before. I can't imagine how it could happen. Jesus breaks some bread and hands it to me. He then breaks off a piece of fish and hands it to me. At that point, it certainly must not have appeared to be enough to give to hungry people. I think of myself walking up to a large man who hasn't eaten all day, with a sardine-size piece of fish and half a biscuit. I'm sure I would feel timid. But out of sheer obedience, as I stretch out my hand to give him food, something amazing happens. It multiplies into an amount that would overfill a plate. So much, the Bible says, that everyone got all they wanted to eat. I can see myself going back with excitement for another morsel. Gradually, I would become more confident in this food distribution ministry. Amazed, I would start passing it out as fast as I could, knowing there would always be more. Maybe I would begin dancing as I passed it out. Maybe I'd try a behind-the-back toss of bread into the hands of a smiling child. I would be thinking how fun it is to serve the Lord.

> *God's power works through us to the point that what once seemed intimidating becomes a task worth celebrating.*

This is a picture of what it is like to be used as an instrument of the Holy Spirit. Somehow, as we are obedient,

God's power works through us to the point that what once seemed intimidating becomes a task worth celebrating.

Moving in the Holy Spirit doesn't happen because we dial up some super power; it happens when we "dial down" to listen, recognize, and move in step in a natural way as the Holy Spirit leads. We learn to train our senses to discern and bless what the Holy Spirit is doing, offering ourselves to participate in that miracle at His leading. It doesn't matter if we're clumsy, or don't appear "anointed." We know that we are just delivering a package and it's not about the delivery person. We sometimes describe it as being a midwife. We don't step in and brashly say, "We are here to take out that baby." No, we are here to bless the power at work and facilitate as an assistant. As we encounter needs, either naturally or beyond our human ability to meet, we learn to do like Jesus did: lift our eyes to heaven, expecting to recognize what God is doing and step out. We love to pray, "Come, Holy Spirit," and like a surfer stepping into a wave, adjust accordingly in order to move in His power. The key is being willing to take the step of faith when He leads.

I remember learning the difference between performing and partnering as a young man. I had been reading the story of Peter, when he said to the man lying by the gate of the temple: *"Silver and gold I do not have, but what I do have, I give you: In the name of Jesus Christ of Nazareth, rise up and walk"* (Acts 3:6 NKJV). Then taking the man's hand, Peter lifted him up. One night after a church service, I came across a woman in a wheelchair. I was hyped and marched up to her to do my best "man-of-faith-and-power" impersonation. But as I reached out to take her hand, I noticed that underneath her lap-blanket she had no legs. My faith shriveled. Embarrassed, I just apologized and shrunk away, not wanting to ever try to pray like that again.

A short time later, though, in the foyer of another church, I was talking with a lady who had been in an accident and was on crutches. I had no intention of praying for her. We were just visiting when all of the sudden there was a nudge in my heart. I just knew that I knew: God's spirit was moving on her for healing. Reluctantly, without really feeling any faith, I asked if I could pray for her. To my amazement, the power of God moved visibly upon her. She threw down her crutches and began hopping around. She was completely healed, and even gave me her crutches as a souvenir. I felt like the woodpecker in a story I heard, who was pecking on a tree, when right above it a lightning bolt suddenly hit and the tree split in half. The shocked woodpecker said to himself, "I never knew I had that kind of power!" The truth is, we don't. All our power is in Jesus when we move in partnership with His Holy Spirit and we are dependent on Him.

I remember a pastor telling me as a young man to be open as never before to the move of the Holy Spirit. He said God had shown him, "I am going to do surprising things, in surprising ways, through surprising people, so don't be surprised." I believe with all of my heart that this applies to all of us. You are one of those surprising people He is going to use in surprising ways, so don't be surprised.

This way of moving with the Holy Spirit is not only fundamental in seeing God use us in areas like the gift of healing, but in how we partner with God in ordinary things like sharing a testimony, serving a lunch, or deciding how to raise our kids. Later in the story, Jesus unpacks how they can walk in His power when He

> *You are one of those surprising people He is going to use in surprising ways, so don't be surprised.*

makes the comment, *"The Spirit gives life; the flesh counts for nothing. The words I have spoken to you — they are full of the Spirit and life"* (John 6:63 NIV).

If we are going to see the abundance of God revealed in every dimension of our lives, we must learn to continuously switch from relying on ourselves and "lean in" to the power of the Holy Spirit. The disciples had their plans for getting things done and meeting the needs of the people – they were going to send them to the surrounding villages. It would've been so easy for them to miss God's plans had they leaned on their own understanding. Jesus clearly states *"...without Me you can do nothing"* (John 15:5 NKJV). We might do human things apart from Him, but we can't do anything that will make an eternal difference in people's lives.

So many Christians are frustrated and burned out because they are busy, maybe even for the Lord. But they fail to learn how to work, not just for the Lord but *from* the Lord, out of God's wallet of strength and power. Someone said, "When we work, God waits, but when we're willing to wait, God works."

Warren Buffet said in another context, "Sometimes it's not how fast you row your boat. It's how fast the stream is going."[38] God wants us to operate in the river of the Holy Spirit. We may be great paddlers and hard workers, but ultimately our human strength can never produce God's fruit. He wants us to continuously reposition ourselves, identifying that we are completely looking to Him for His leading. He wants us to grasp the paradox that reigning comes through resting, relying not on our own efforts/initiatives, but God's.

This was illustrated with my kids when they were quite young. My 4-year-old son Joey was frustrated during a family game of baseball because he kept striking out. Finally, I asked him, "Joey, what if we hit together?" He agreed, so as my older son pitched the ball, I came behind him and put my hands over his on the bat. The pitch came and when we swung, we hit a home run. He was so proud, pumping his little fist as he ran around the bases.

Over and over, the Lord wants us to acknowledge our dependence on the Holy Spirit – that we find strength through

Him and not ourselves. Wayne Cordeiro said, "We don't forget that we are Christians. We forget that we are humans, and that one oversight alone can debilitate the potential of our future."[39] We easily fall into the pattern of playing God.

We readily take the kind of detour that Abraham took, when instead of waiting on God, he decided to help God out and take Hagar as his concubine to conceive the promised child (Gen. 16). This simply delayed God's plan. It was only as he and Sarah owned the impossibility of producing a child in their own strength, and abandoned themselves to trust the promise of God, that the miracle happened.

People who live in the abundance of God are constantly learning that it's "*not by might nor by power, but by My Spirit, says the Lord*" (Zech. 4:6). We do this by faithfully trusting in what only God can do.

I sensed God calling me to preach when I was just a little boy. The first time I felt certain that my life's calling truly was to preach, my childish reaction was the same as it had been years before: I told the Lord, "No way!" I am by personality a shy person. In fact, I was put in the slow reading group as an elementary student, not because I couldn't read well, but because when I was asked to read out loud, I froze. The thought of spending my life speaking in public terrified me. I basically had told the Lord "anything but that."

A shift came one day when I was walking across the park as a young Christian. There was a large group of hippies in a big circle drinking beer and smoking pot. It suddenly became clear that I was to go to them and tell them about Jesus. Of course, I was terrified. The thought of doing that felt like walking off a cliff. In my total weakness, I approached this group of around 30 in sheer obedience, got their attention and began to speak. To my dismay, my "Mickey Mouse" voice came out. They snickered and told me to go away, someone even threw a beer can. Then suddenly to my shock, the Holy Spirit rose up in me, my voice changed and I began to boldly share the gospel. The crowd went into confusion, many scattered and some stayed. In the end, several people huddled with me to pray a prayer of salvation. In retrospect, I understood why the Lord made me such a shy person. In everything I would try to share about the Lord, my call was to move from relying on my strength to leaning completely into the Holy Spirit.

APPLICATION

Jesus brings the resources of heaven to meet the needs of Earth by using ordinary people to do extraordinary things. The disciples were ordinary people with ordinary abilities and vision. They walked through an ordinary large crowd, served ordinary food in an ordinary basket. Yet, the ordinary became extraordinary.

As you walk through your ordinary day, which of the following would **most** welcome God to change the ordinary into extraordinary?

Working from the Lord	Working for the Lord
Performing	Dialing-down
Partnering	Being a great paddler
Fortress mindset	Force mindset
Ability	Obedience

A "normal" Christian is someone who, by the power of the Holy Spirit attempts to do what Jesus would do for people, wherever they are.

Chapter 13

AN ABUNDANCE MINDSET FOR MINISTRY/ PRIESTS AND KINGS

"Jesus took the five loaves and two fish, looked up toward heaven, and blessed them. Then, breaking the loaves into pieces, He gave the bread to the disciples, who distributed it to the people. They all ate as much as they wanted..."(Matt. 14:19b-20a NLT).

Jesus brought a whole new "wineskin" to how we think about ministry. As mentioned, there is no more important way for the resources of heaven to be released on Earth than through the awakening of every member of God's church to their ministry potential. The same power that raised Jesus resides in us: unstoppable, world-changing power and love (Rom. 8:11). It is reported that one of the Japanese generals responsible for the attack on Pearl Harbor was quoted later as saying, "I fear we may have awakened a sleeping giant."[40] There is no sleeping giant like the church.

> *The same power that raised Jesus resides in us: unstoppable, world-changing power and love.*

In the previous chapter, I pointed out the importance of removing the lids in our thinking regarding who is qualified to minister and what their potential is for ministry. Let's further address the implications of where and with whom people with an abundance mindset can minister.

In this passage, we see Jesus laying a foundation for how He wanted ministry to unfold. He came to not just do the ministry but to multiply the ministry. He provided this example for all church leaders to follow. In Ephesians 4:12, we learn that the responsibility of apostles, prophets, evangelists, pastors, and teachers is to equip God's people to do His work and build up the church. The key function as pastors or ministry leaders is not to just minister to people but to switch roles with them as quickly as possible so that *the people* are doing the ministry. God doesn't want to only anoint special individuals, but all members of His body to function together.

He also wants to remove the limitations of *where* the church ministers. The church is not merely a building. We may say our church is on 1605 South Valley Drive. But that is only true when we gather for worship. But where is our church the rest of the time? We are scattered everywhere, being the church at the grocery store, the electric company, in school, in our neighborhoods and our homes.

> *Where is our church? We are scattered everywhere, being the church at the grocery store, the electric company, in school, in our neighborhoods and our homes.*

Multiplication in ministry happens when we transition from a "me" to a "we" mindset. I believe the Lord doesn't want to empower only a certain few people in the church, but wants to empower entire churches and businesses, schools and all kinds of organizations to multiply His kingdom. The goal of ministry is not simply getting people into heaven, but bringing heaven to the people, in cities, marketplaces, or wherever they can be reached.

This was highlighted in planting our present church. In 1997, we made a decision to resign from the fantastic church we were leading in El Paso. There was this deep burden for the nations, and we thought perhaps the Lord would have us focus on the Philippines, in particular. To our surprise, the Lord spoke very clearly to us about moving to Las Cruces and planting His church there. Las Cruces is about 40 miles up the road and it hadn't been on our radar as the place God would call us as "missionaries." It became obvious to us that our mission wasn't about leaving the U.S. or the American church; it was about taking the church to the nations.

We felt a deep calling to plant a church completely from a missionary point of view, a church that would "give our very best to those who had the very least." We determined that our first measure of success would be our impact on the most marginalized of society. He wanted us to be an organization truly focused on our "nonmembers": the lost, the last, and the least, here and around the world.

We became convinced that another measure of success would be based not on our seating capacity but our sending capacity. I have sometimes joked with the church that my vision for most of them is to leave – not *from* us but as part of us – to multiply elsewhere what they have received here. Jesus spoke of this mindset when he said, *"Freely, you have received, freely give"* (Matt. 10:8). As our motto says, we are "a neighborhood church on a worldwide mission."

Perhaps just as important, I felt He wanted my focus not so much on who I could reach as a missionary evangelist, but on how and who we could equip our members to reach. It was clear that our "success" would be based on how we could awaken "the sleeping giant." This focus has resulted in planting several churches in the U.S. and overseas, partnering with hidden heroes, and taking well over 2,000 people on short-term mission trips. Equally important has been helping people see their mission calling in their everyday world. We believe everyone has different spheres into which God wants to bring His kingdom.

Many people view missions mostly in geographic terms. To be called as a missionary is considered a call to leave your vocation and move somewhere to serve God and people. Although this is certainly the case for some, for others it presents a limited perspective of their mission potential. As with our story of the loaves and fishes, so often our "mission" is right in front of us and we just don't see it or we are wishing it would go away.

In the Sermon on the Mount, Jesus described mission as influence. Mission is being "salt and light" – letting your light so shine before people in your sphere of influence that they are drawn towards glorifying God (Matt. 5:13-16).

In reality, a missionary isn't necessarily someone who changes their career but someone who changes their vision. In Genesis 15:5, we read that Abraham was confused as to how he would ever fulfill his calling to be a person through whom all the nations of the world would be blessed. In a life-changing moment that switched his thinking, the Lord told him to get outside of his tent, look at the stars and try to count them. God revealed that Abraham's impact on the entire world would begin with his influence in his tiny family of himself and Sarah, before they even had a son. Some never find their mission because they are trapped in small assumptions about their purpose and mission in life.

I like the story of a third-grade teacher who wanted her students to grasp the enormity of the universe. She gave the class an assignment to go into their backyard that night and count as many stars as they could. The next day, she asked the children how many they had seen. One girl said 200. Another said, "I couldn't count because there were like millions."

She asked, "Johnny, how many did you count?"

"Three," he said.

"Really, Johnny? That's hardly any."

"I know teacher, but you have to understand, I have a very small backyard."

You can't overemphasize the importance of people grasping the size of God's vision for their life. The size of our vision helps determine the size of our impact.

Someone said, "Missions isn't crossing the sea, it is seeing the cross."[41] We must break out of a self-absorbed perspective and ask the Lord to help us see what He sees when He looks at the world. One of the reasons we eagerly urge our people to go on mission trips is because many of us, like myself, need to move outside our box, with our attention focused on others in order to really see what He sees (Phil. 2:3-7).

As we shift towards God's heart for people around us, we discover that our mission includes not just a geographic place but a **stream of influence**. There are many spheres of influence beyond the "church" world: education, health care, entertainment and media, the arts, government, law enforcement, family and many more. Throughout the Bible, God not only anointed prophets and priests but people like Joseph and Lydia, who received an anointing for business; like Esther and Daniel for government. Even a man named Bezalel was anointed as a craftsman to make artistic hangings and designs for the tabernacle (Exod. 36).

God has many platforms for displaying His glory, and all are mission fields as well. Who better to reach engineers than other engineers? Because of innovations like the internet and global markets, almost any area of service can easily provide not only local but global opportunities to advance the kingdom of God. We are especially seeing the gospel advance through non-traditional avenues to reach the 3,000 or so unreached people groups.

What turns an ordinary or "secular" job into a mission is not a title or a position, but a clear belief in a heavenly purpose. I have a friend who told me, "I am a missionary for Jesus Christ in the public school system. The cool thing is the El Paso Public School District pays my salary." One business owner who changed from entrepreneur to business owner for Jesus, described the switch in his heart this way:

> *What turns an ordinary or "secular" job into a mission is not a title or a position, but a clear belief in a heavenly purpose.*

"My bottom line has changed. In business, you usually think of the bottom line as the profit you can make to run the business. As I've come to understand, God has blessed me to be a blessing. My bottom line is to continually consider how God's blessing on me and my business can be leveraged to help others and further expand the sharing of the gospel with the world."

I believe that God not only places people in the market-place, He anoints them in those positions in the same way He anoints a pastor or an evangelist in theirs. In I Corinthians 12, Paul is sharing about the gifts of the Holy Spirit, including prophecy and miracles. In verses 4-6, we see there is not only a variety of gifts but a myriad of ways these gifts flow and are exercised by people in different contexts.

For example, God anoints people with the ability to create wealth. In Deuteronomy 8:18 NKJV, Moses tells the people, *"And you shall remember the Lord your God, for it is He who gives you power to get wealth..."*

Eric Liddell, the Olympic athlete turned missionary said, "I feel the pleasure of God when I run."[42] I know business leaders who sense the pleasure of God when creating wealth. Some have felt that was unspiritual and couldn't possibly be from God because of the warnings in the Bible against the love of money. Yet, there is plenty of Biblical evidence that God would have us see money as a tool that can produce amazing ministry. In Luke 16:9, in the parable of the steward, Jesus speaks of the ability to invest money for the purpose of making eternal friendships, or as a treasure to help people find eternal life in Jesus.[43] I heard one person say, "Without a vision the people perish, but without provision the vision perishes." Resourcing the outreach of Christ is a key ministry. I believe God wants to give some people that "Joseph anointing" to capture carnal cash and turn it into kingdom currency.

Peter Wagner, a former professor at Fuller Seminary, shared a prophecy that resonated with me. He believed that there would be the greatest transfer of wealth in the history of the world for the causes of the kingdom. Just as Proverbs 13:22 NIV states, "*a sinner's wealth is stored up for the righteous.*" I believe this is one method God is using to fuel the present, great end-times harvest. What a blessing when people truly are called and see this as a ministry.

R.G. Le Tourneau was an example of a modern Joseph. In the early part of the last century, he felt pulled to do more for God. He went to his pastor, Reverend Devol, for advice. Le Tourneau thought that anyone who was wholly committed to Christ had to become a pastor or a missionary to truly fulfill the great commission. After prayer with his pastor, R.G. was shocked to hear Rev. Devol state, 'God needs businessmen too.' With this revelation, Le Tourneau immediately began to consider his business as a partnership with God. In 1935, with a prospering manufacturing business, R.G. and his wife, Evelyn, transitioned to a 90/10 split with the Lord: 90 percent went to the Lord and 10 percent went to R.G. and Evelyn.[44]

LeTourneau was largely responsible for the invention and development of many types of earthmoving machines used today.[45] He later established Le Tourneau University, with a vision of "Claiming every workplace in every nation as our mission field".[46] His compassion and evangelistic investments have changed the lives and eternities of millions.

This anointing to be a missionary influence in different streams of society is not only true of business, but all other areas as well. George Washington Carver achieved this in the world of science and agriculture. Born a slave who became a scientist after the Civil War, he was credited with helping to revolutionize and restore the Southern U.S. economy when it needed it most.[47] Every day, George Washington Carver would pray not only for wisdom but revelation in his scientific pursuits and experiments. He evangelized and shared his love of God and science with as many people as possible. [48]

He once said, "I love to think of nature as the unlimited broadcasting station, through which God speaks every hour to us if we will only tune in."[49]

He recounted, "When I was young, I said to God, 'God, tell me the mystery of the universe.'"

But God answered, "That knowledge is reserved for Me alone."

So, I said, "God, tell me the mystery of the peanut."

Then God said, "Well George, that's more nearly your size."[50]

Carver went on to discover more than 300 uses for the peanut as well as 500 other products.[51]

Beyond recognizing the Christian's call to missions, an abundance mindset grasps how our gifts and abilities are designed to be weaved in multifaceted partnerships that multiply their impact. Our assignment is to connect and flow in partnership with other people and organizations, where we discover the explosive potential of our individual gifts and anointings.

Jesus says, *"When two of you get together on anything at all on Earth and make a prayer of it, My Father in heaven goes into action. And when two or three of you are together because of Me, you can be sure that I'll be there"* (Matt 18:19 MSG).

This mission of reaching out to the world with the gospel is described almost as an assembly line process. Paul said, "One sows, one waters, and one reaps..." (I Cor. 3:6-9). To make the mission successful, the process must be fueled by a harvest team of believers through multiplied acts of prayer, providing, participating, and partnering.

God says in Amos 3:3 NKJV, *"Can two walk together, unless they are agreed?"* According to Pastor Gerald Brooks, the original word for agreement is a divine appointment. Walking together with certain people for the advancement of God's kingdom is a calling in itself. God places us in strategic relationships to accomplish even more for His glory together than we could individually.

God is doing this all over the world. Matthew Barnett said that God has destined to build His kingdom through the gift of friendships and relationships. Throughout the world, God is moving to put together teams, sometimes organizationally or sometimes for specific partnerships.

We like to say, the greater the team the greater the dream. You can pursue a small dream on your own. If you want to climb a small hill at a park, you can go it alone. But to climb Mount Everest, you need a great team. God is pulling people together across traditional lines for Mount Everest-sized dreams and visions. We need to recognize and develop our God-designed and assigned connections.

> *To climb Mount Everest, you need a great team.*

One area where these partnerships are especially crucial is between marketplace leaders and ministry-place leaders. The Bible has numerous examples of these two roles and speaks of His people as "kings and priests" (Rev. 1:5-6 NKJV). In Old Testament Israel, kings were to lead the nation in justice, commerce and war. Priests were to lead with a focus on the temple and on hearing and discerning the prophetic voice of God. Specially designed partnerships between kings and priests existed between Nathan and David, Samuel and Saul, Mordecai and Esther, Moses and Aaron, Zechariah and Zerubbabel. When these partnerships were functioning effectively, the impact of both leaders and their sphere of influence increased dramatically.

This pattern continued in the early church. The apostles focused on, and dedicated themselves to, teaching the Word of God and prayer, while marketplace leaders in the church organized its social, outreach and organizational functions. In Acts 6:2-4, 7 NKJV, we see that because they maintained their roles and partnered effectively, the outcome was: *"The word of God spread, and the number of disciples multiplied greatly in Jerusalem."*

Over the years, I have found that, as a ministry leader, whenever I was able to properly identify strategic partnerships with marketplace leaders, there has been a synergy and complementary increase of effectiveness for the kingdom of God in both our streams. Among the team of "kings" I work with, I have come to find many gifts that balance each other and have helped us attain higher levels. Whereas I am gifted at spiritual vision, they are gifted with capturing and managing Earthly provision. Where I have dreams, they have schemes. Where I create prayer strategies, they create production strategies. Where I move in revelation, they move in wisdom. Where I have a call to create spiritual impact, their partnership in communities around the world demonstrates God's kingdom in areas such as economic, educational, or healthcare impact. Where I preach the good news of salvation and release people from spiritual poverty, they bring systems to address physical poverty.

Unfortunately, so often "kings and priests" have struggled to unite. In some cases, kings feel spiritually intimidated by the priests, and priests feel intimidated by the material wealth or business influence of the kings. Sometimes we remain separated because of how differently we relate, instead of discovering how those differences make us all so much better. I believe an abundance mindset includes commitment and confidence to build powerful relationships of mutual respect and love across innate differences.

I heard a funny story of a very organized, hard-working lady who fell in love with a preacher. She felt so blessed when she heard him preach that the anointing would just fall upon her. He was so attracted to her, not only by how pretty she was, but by how industrious she was. She had a great business and a beautifully ordered house. They eventually married, but soon there were problems. She was neat and tidy, and he wasn't so much. When things needed to be fixed and organized, he tried but was poor at it. At one point, the lady was so frustrated her anger began to rise. But when she looked at her husband across the room, she imagined seeing him in the pulpit. Before losing her temper, she cried out, "Preach, honey! Preach!" It's good when we can turn our differences into partnerships of mutual effectiveness.

For these partnerships to work, it is crucial to understand what partnership really is. It is not networking. It isn't just sharing a common goal; partnership is sharing a *common heart*.

I have found that in the kingdom of God, contracts, though perhaps sometimes necessary, are not enough for partnership. Covenant is required.

Covenant relationship is a higher level of agreement which is committed to Jesus first, honoring and adding value to the other; offering accountability and transparency. In a practical way, this often means being willing to take the time to grow together and sense our calling to serve.

So much is written in the Bible about the priority of creating partnerships of one heart, one mind and one spirit, because it is where the greatest challenge in advancing God's kingdom lies. I have a friend who used to say the ministry would be so incredible if it weren't for people. Learning how to relate and work alongside different kinds of people is challenging, especially cross-culturally, but it is key to growing the kingdom.

An abundance mindset asserts that in Christ walls tumble. The spiritual heart-connection is so great that we audaciously declare we are one as Jesus and the Father are one (Eph 2:14-16). Someone said, "Blood is thicker than water, but spirit is thicker than blood." It is through taking up our cross to serve others that we find grace for this.

A pastor who was in a covenant partnership helping other pastors, shared this line, "My dream is to make your dream come true." I believe this statement reflects the heart of Jesus when He said to His disciples, *"Very truly I tell you, whoever believes in me will do the works I have been doing, and they will do even greater things than these, because I am going to the Father"* (John 14:12 NIV). Jesus gave His disciples His ministry, not to just do what He had done but to be able to see them do even greater works.

I am convinced that one of the key words God has for His people in these last days is *alignment*. He is calling all His people with their multifaceted gifts, interests, and abilities to strategically align (like dominoes set in chain-reaction formation). How much wiser it is to complete than to compete. The pipeline of revival will be set for a gusher as kings and priests (scientists and evangelists, inventors and intercessors, entrepreneurs and apostles, bank tellers and miracle workers) realize how much better we are together. Jesus urged us that unity would mean the world will see His full glory, and the nations will come to Him (John 17:21).

APPLICATION

There are many spheres of influence beyond the "church" world. Write several spheres of influence you have outside of "church" and ways God could use your influence.

What turns an ordinary or "secular" job into a mission is not a title or a position, but a clear belief in a heavenly purpose. Try writing your job description from God's view. (You could include various roles such as student, spouse, parent...)

My purpose is:
My goal is:
My daily plan to reach my goal and fulfill my purpose is:

To climb Mount Everest, you need a great team. Describe a mountain (physical or spiritual) that you have climbed. Who helped you? In what ways do you see yourself aligning with a harvest team of believers to accomplish Mount Everest-sized dreams?

How much better we are together.

Chapter 14

LIVING OUT OF THE OVERFLOW OF CONTENTMENT

"Do not work for food that spoils, but for food that endures to eternal life, which the Son of Man will give you" (John 6:27 NIV).

"I am the Bread of Life. Your ancestors ate the manna in the wilderness, yet they died. I am the living bread that came down from heaven. Whoever eats this bread will live forever" (John 6:48-49; 51 NIV).

Living a life of abundance doesn't come from our effort or a sense of moral obligation. It comes from the overflow of a heart that is full and content. It comes from a heart that has refocused its desires from things of the Earth onto Jesus, our delight.

As we read the end of the story in John chapter 6, Jesus makes clear that the real point of the miracle wasn't satisfying their physical hunger but redirecting the appetites of their heart from the cravings of this world to Jesus Himself, the Bread of Life. Everything shared about Jesus in the book of John was for people to believe in Him, and in believing in Him, find Life.

The day of the miracle ended, but interest in what Jesus provided for the people didn't end. The next day, when the crowd realized Jesus had left, they got into their boats in search of Jesus.

John says they had plans to force Him to become their king (John 6:15). They saw what looked like a really sweet deal. Jesus could be their ticket to a never-ending all-you-can-eat buffet. Much like people do today, they were seeking God as a means to their ends; pretending to follow God, but really hoping that God would follow them to help fulfill their agenda. More than once, I have noticed a young man suddenly appear at church sitting beside one of our young ladies. Sometimes their interest isn't to give themselves to God, but to use Him or church to get something for themselves.

Jesus refused their offer to be king and did all He could to redirect their hunger and desire toward what will ultimately satisfy. As He did with a woman at a well earlier in the book, He points out that pursuing material things to satisfy the deep spiritual cravings of the human heart never works. Like Israel in the wilderness, they got their bread but missed God. They had full stomachs but empty hearts. They allowed themselves to be bound by one of the worse forms of a scarcity mindset: **consumerism** – belief that one's fulfillment and meaning comes from money, success, recognition, power or fame. The bitter fruit of a consumer mindset is ultimately discontentment.

Author John Cheever noted, "The main emotion of the adult Northeastern American who has had all the advantages of wealth, education and culture is disappointment."[52] We live in a culture that exploits our tendencies towards dissatisfaction. The marketing industry spends billions of dollars creating strategies to convince us that we urgently need one more product to truly be fulfilled. I recently heard that there are now more than 430 brands of shampoo, all in some way promising ultimate hair happiness. We can meet every hair desire. We can wash it, condition it, curl it, straighten it, color it, shape it, add to it, and if necessary "Rogaine" it.

The problem is we are spiritual, eternal beings controlled by fleshly desires. There is nothing physical that can satisfy the longing of our heart. But there is One who can fill us, so that our joy doesn't depend on the rewards of this world. The good things of life become icing on the cake but aren't required for true contentment. Christ's contentment empowers us to become overflowing rivers, enabling us to focus on the needs of others instead of becoming a stagnant pond, settling on just our own needs.

John Piper points to this key switch that produces over-flowing contentment: trading our focus from the desires of our flesh for the One who is the desire of our heart. A person who lives in discontentment looks to some *thing* to satisfy; a person who finds contentment looks to *Someone* to satisfy. Piper wrote:

> "The great sin of the world is not that the human race has failed to work for God to increase his glory, but that we've failed to delight in God so as to reflect his glory. God's glory is most reflected in us when we are most delighted in Him. When God is most glorified, man is most satisfied. When man is most satisfied, God is most glorified."[53]

Jesus taught that if we will but 'eat' of Him, even if who you are or what you have on the outside may not change, your joy and satisfaction on the inside will be complete.

Paul revealed in Philippians 4:11-13 that he had learned the secret of contentment. The word contentment means sufficiency. It means to be and to have plenty too much in any circumstance. Incredibly, Paul was in a Roman prison when he declared that he was just as full and complete in chains with nothing as when he was in prosperous circumstances. I was amazed reading Richard Wurmbrand's story in the book *Tortured for Christ.* Richard was a pastor imprisoned for his faith in Romania during the Soviet era. He wrote, "Alone in a cell; cold, hungry, and in rags, I danced for joy every night. Sometimes I was so filled with joy that I felt I would burst if I didn't give expression to it."[54]

When Jesus fills your heart, the other good things in life are a bonus. I read about a precious Quaker brother who was observed going to his cupboard and finding only some bread and broth to eat. He began weeping and, lifting up his hands, exclaimed:

> *When Jesus fills your heart, the other good things in life are a bonus.*

"Imagine all of this and Jesus too." J.H. Jowett, an influential British Preacher, said "The real measure of our wealth is how much we should be worth if we lost all our money."[55]

How do we partake of Jesus in a way that we are truly satisfied? The first key is redirecting our desires from what our mind tells us we need and switching them to the One who is always enough, all that we need. It means we reach for Jesus's presence.

The other day, the frustration of driving in traffic made me angry. My mind said "To be happy, you need to be in traffic that parts open for you, with drivers who aren't crazy." I realized in that moment the frustration I felt was really a hunger for more of Jesus. I was hungering for God's peace and patience. Patience has been defined as an inner confidence that Jesus has provided everything I need for my present happiness. As He always is, Jesus was waiting to be invited into my situation. As I sought Him in worship, God filled my heart. The Bible says, even if I make my bed in hell, He is there (Ps. 139:8). Did you ever feel like traffic resembled hell?

The second key in redirecting our desires is recognizing what it is we are seeking. Discontentment is the driving desire to get my way because I deserve it or need it to be fulfilled. I can even become manipulative and try to use God for my own ends. Jesus says, "Don't work for food that perishes." He is directing us to check our motives. What are you demanding in this situation for yourself? Are you expecting God to follow you or are you willing to follow God? Are you seeking or demanding a gift from God, or are you willing to let your surrendered heart be a gift for God, the surrender that says, "I embrace Your best for me, even if I don't see it now"? This switches our desire from what we want to what He wants in the situation. Breakthrough comes when we want what He is giving.

Third, contentment comes as we delight in the Lord by rejoicing and giving thanks in our circumstances, for in all ways, He is enough. Psalms 37:4 says, *"Delight in the Lord and He shall give you the desires of your heart"* (NJKV). Someone said that there is a place where you can live with all the longings and desires of your heart continually met. But if your longing is for anything other than Jesus, you are not yet in that place. That place is where Jesus is truly the first and ultimate desire of your heart. When Jesus is your "magnificent obsession" you will have all the possessions you need to be utterly fulfilled. Another way to think about it is to realize that there are two kinds of people: Those who see happiness based on getting what they want, and those who see happiness based on being grateful for what they already have.

> *There are two kinds of people: Those who see happiness based on getting what they want, and those who see happiness based on being grateful for what they already have.*

People who are waiting to receive something or obtain a goal in order to become grateful end up chasing the wind. Like drinking sea water to satisfy their thirst, fulfillment is a mirage of what they really long for.

Have you ever heard people talk like this?
"When I turn sixteen, I will be happy."
But when they're sixteen they say, "When I graduate from high school, I will be happy."
Then it's, "When I find a boyfriend, I will be happy."
Then, "When I get rid of this boyfriend, I will be happy."
"When I get married and have kids, I will be happy."
But then, "When these kids finally grow up and leave, I will be happy."

No, they won't because happiness isn't something; it is *Someone*.

> *Happiness isn't something; it is Someone.*

The Bible beautifully states in Psalm 16:11 that in His presence is fullness of joy; at His right hand are pleasures evermore. People who are content with Jesus find themselves tapped into God as the result. They find an overflow from heaven that touches and ministers to the sorrows and needs of people around them. They naturally become thermostats instead of thermometers, changing the atmosphere wherever they are. The more you desire Him, the more you are filled, the more you are filled, the more you will desire Him.

HERE IS A PRAYER TO SWITCH MY DESIRE FROM SOMETHING TO OUR BLESSED SOMEONE

"Oh, precious Jesus, You are all I need; You are truly the 'All' I ever wanted. I acknowledge that every place I feel empty, stressed, anxious, disappointed, is a place where Your presence wants to come and fill. I set aside and refuse to carve out a broken cistern. I refuse to accept any substitute for your joy. I refuse to settle for a good mood when I can be filled with the love of my good, good Father.

I surrender my agenda and opinions about what I need. I refuse to live for my wants and refuse in any way to try to convince You to promote my will. Today, I don't demand You give me gifts, but I come to offer myself as a gift to You. I know if I lose my life, I will find it. If I offer myself as a living sacrifice, I will be consumed with a fire of glory.

I choose right now the greatest privilege of my life: to delight in You, to make You and let You be the treasure and delight of my heart. You are more beautiful than I can describe, more precious than all I can imagine. Open my heart and spiritual eyes to see how vast and great Your love and goodness are for me. I accept now that I have plenty too much in You for fullness of joy that will saturate every corner of my life. Oh Lord, filled with You, I will take my eyes off myself and focus on You. In this place of rest, everything I do will be from joy and satisfaction. I will not have to do even one thing for it. With You in me, Jesus, I overflow.

Chapter 15

Eternal Perspective/ Thinking As Big As Heaven

"Do not work for food that spoils, but for food that endures to eternal life, which the Son of Man will give you" (John 6:27 NIV).

"...but whoever feeds on this bread will live forever" (John 6:58 NIV).

Jesus urged the people to let their experience of a one-time miracle lead them to a lifetime of transformation, by switching their thinking from an earthly perspective to an eternal perspective. To be a person of abundance who taps into all that God has for us we must allow the bigness of the eternal to invade the smallness of our preoccupation with this temporal life. Our preoccupation with earth stuff can blind us to the power, wisdom, courage, hope, strength, and faith of an eternal perspective.

In the Sermon on the Mount, Jesus spoke about storing up riches in Heaven instead of on Earth: *"If your eyes* (focus) *are healthy, your whole body will be full of light"* (Matt. 6:22 NIV). People who view life beyond their physical expiration date grasp a perspective that fills them with power and opportunity. Let me point out a few ways an eternal perspective brings God's abundance to you and through you.

An eternal perspective gives us comfort and courage to crash through barriers of fear, discouragement and doubt in times of suffering. In Hebrews 11, we read a list of heroes in the "hall of faith" that includes martyrs and people who overcame unimaginable suffering and made a great difference for God. They knew they were just foreigners and strangers in this world, and their longing was for a 'better country' – a heavenly one (Heb. 11:13-16).

It makes all the difference if, rather than seeing this life as your final destination and putting all of your eggs in this physical basket, you see life as Ron Hutchcraft described it, "a long night in a cheap hotel." Imagine today as a single day on a mission trip, an opportunity to make a difference on your way home, where *"Eye has not seen, nor ear heard, nor have entered into the heart of man the things which God has prepared for those who love Him"* (I Cor. 2:9 NKJV).

> *Imagine today as a single day on a mission trip, an opportunity to make a difference on your way home.*

> *The more you focus on your destination and not your difficulties, the more promising the future looks and the smaller all the problems in your life become.*

It was this perspective in the early days that caused martyrs about to be mauled, to run toward the lions, singing a song of praise to God. It drew them to the cemeteries every Easter to dance in celebration on the graves of their loved ones, who they knew were dancing with Jesus. The more you focus on your destination and not your difficulties, the more promising the future looks and the smaller all the problems in your life become.

Jesus gives you a picture of heaven to keep in your wallet. Your capacity to keep gazing on that image completely changes the score on how you handle adversity and rise to occasions where courage is required to bring the Kingdom. Florence Chadwick was the first American woman to swim across the English Channel. On her first, unsuccessful, attempt to cross the grueling 21 miles, she faced a very foggy day. Just a short distance shy of the shore, she cried "uncle" and called to be rescued. She later explained, "All I could see was the fog....I think if I could have seen the shore, I would have made it."[56]

In the early part of the last century, missionaries Henry Morrison and his wife were returning on a ship from Africa after spending decades there, living in terribly hard conditions and losing family members to disease. On the same ship, President Roosevelt was traveling back from a safari. When they arrived at New York Harbor, the president was greeted by a band playing and thousands of people waving flags, welcoming him home. As the missionaries disembarked, they felt demoralized that there was no one waiting for them. Walking down the street, feeling the sting of that moment, the Lord sweetly spoke to Henry's heart, "Don't worry son, you're not home yet."[57] Earth is just a stopover on the way to a welcome party that will make Teddy Roosevelt's welcome seem laughable.

Paul tells us that he considered the sufferings of this life not worthy to be compared with the glory that we shall see (Rom. 8:18). As we suffer and deal with the horrible injustices that fill our "I don't understand why this is allowed to happen" filing cabinet of questions, we have assurance of a moment which will rectify and make sense of everything that breaks our heart down here.

About the day of Resurrection, Dostoevsky said that we will see everything suddenly made right that didn't *even out* here. He said:

> "I believe like a child that suffering will be healed and made up for, that all the humiliating absurdity of human contradictions will vanish like a pitiful mirage, like the despicable fabrication of the impotent and infinitely small Euclidean mind of man, that in

the world's finale, at the moment of eternal harmony, something so precious will come to pass that it will suffice for all hearts, for the comforting of all resentments, for the atonement of all the crimes of humanity, for all the blood that they've shed; that it will make it not only possible to forgive but to justify all that has happened."[58]

Joni Eareckson Tada has lived her life as a quadriplegic in a wheelchair as the result of a diving accident when she was a teenager. She has been one of the most inspirational Christian leaders of our era, preaching the gospel and giving hope to millions through speaking, writing and painting with her teeth. Joni leads a ministry called "Wheels for the World" which provides mobility to immobilized people in impoverished situations.[59] She has also shared honestly about her physical suffering and limitations:

"At the close of the message, the speaker asked everyone to do something unusual. He asked us to push our chairs away from our tables and, if we feel comfortable in doing so, get out of your chair and kneel on the carpeted floor in prayer. Well, I sat there in my wheelchair and I watched as everyone else in the room – there had to be maybe 500 or 600 people — all of them got out of their chairs and they got down on their knees for a brief time of worship. With everyone kneeling in the banquet room, I sat there kind of standing out. I looked around and I was sticking up, way up, the only one sitting there in this huge room. And looking around, I could not stop the tears.

Oh, and I was not crying out of pity. I mean I wasn't crying because I felt strange or different that I was the only one sitting. No, my eyes were wet because it was so beautiful to see everyone kneeling in prayer. And it made me think of the day when I, too, will be able to get up out of this wheelchair on new resurrected legs.

I can't wait for that day because when I get my glorified body, the first thing I'm going to do with my resurrected legs is to fall down on grateful, glorified knees. I will once again have the chance to say with Psalm 95:6, "Come let us bow down in worship, let us kneel before the Lord our Maker."[60]

One of the most helpful suggestions I've heard is to take everything we might be concerned about in life and put them into two categories: *earth stuff* and *eternity stuff.* Before we become upset, terrified, preoccupied, or overwhelmed with anything, we should review which category it's in. For example, the fly on my nose and the bills on my desk are all earth stuff, while spending time with my child in the living room is eternal stuff. The problems and sufferings I'm going through are earth stuff. How I decide to respond and the character lost or formed in me through the struggle is eternal stuff. As I like to say, we have a calling to continually *perspectify* life so that we become servants of the eternal, not victims of our present. I have to do this on a daily basis, especially when I'm driving through traffic.

This eternal perspective helps us determine priorities and seize eternal opportunities. Moses taught us in Psalms 90:12 KJV to pray, *"So teach us to number our days, that we may apply our heart unto wisdom."* This practice of comparing situations and choices that are eternal from ones that are temporal is key to recognizing God's big plan and opportunities for our life.

There is a story of a prank that took place in a New York City department store. One night while it was closed, pranksters snuck in and changed the price tags on all the goods. This was a huge problem, especially in an era before scanning technology. Items that should've been priced at a few dollars were marked in the thousands, while the most expensive diamond watches were priced for pennies. This of course is a picture of what the devil does with the concerns of this world. When we overvalue earthly things, we get blinded to priorities and opportunities that one day we are likely to realize and possibly regret passing up. It has been said that a person on their death bed never asks to see the production reports of their business or clings to their bank statements; they look for their family and to their God. John Wesley said, "I value all things only by the price they shall gain in eternity."[61]

It changes our perspective greatly when we as Christians realize that the real news behind the news we hear every day, of people dying from natural disasters, shootings, etc., is not that people died. It is that seconds after they died, they either began the most glorious or the most unimaginably tragic moment of their existence – an existence that will last forever in either heaven or hell. To really believe this will change the way you look at everything. You will immediately understand the biggest point of life is to make heaven bigger and people's lives better by sharing the words, works and wonders of Christ. It suddenly makes even the smallest opportunity to sow a seed in someone's heart for Jesus the biggest deal of our day.

I was in Zambia sharing the gospel at a crusade on a soccer field. After the invitation time was over, a girl and her friend found me. Jackie was one of the most pitifully sad-looking persons I had ever seen. She was skin and bones, so frail to the point of barely walking. I remember she asked, "Sir, what can Jesus do for someone like me?" She explained that she was a prostitute dying from AIDS, that her entire family had disowned her, and she didn't know what to do. I directed her to *The Healing House,* a ministry we had supported, that assisted people with AIDS. In addition, I got to share the gospel with Jackie. I will never forget the joyful peace shown on her face as she received Christ as her Lord and Savior. Afterwards, I had a whisper from the Lord that was so meaningful to me: "Dale, what Jackie has been through is the only hell she will ever know. There is nothing but glory awaiting her because of that moment of decision."

In Luke 16:9 NLT, Jesus said, *"Here's the lesson. Use your worldly resources to benefit others and make friends. Then, when your possessions are gone, they will welcome you to an eternal home."* It is going to be an incredible experience to walk on the streets of heaven and have Jackie and others welcome us and thank us for being part of the story that brought them to this amazing place.

I believe the greatest point of this life is how the rest of eternity will be different by the choices we make here. To know this gives us both a purpose and a promise. Jesus said, *"Seek first the kingdom of God and His righteousness and all these things shall be added unto you"* (Matt. 6:33). I believe He is saying, do your job, fulfill your responsibilities, be blessed on the journey of life, but in all of it, keep before you the grander vision of making heaven bigger by your life. Remember, what matters most is *names written in the Book of Life* (Luke 10:20; Rev. 20:15). People make such a big deal out of winning the lottery, but when people receive Jesus, they win the incomparable prize of eternal life. What a jackpot!

> *If you keep reaching people for Christ your priority, you will always know you are on the same journey as Jesus.*

If you keep *soul winning* or reaching people for Christ your priority, you will always know you are on the same journey as Jesus. You will have continual assurance that you can ask for the provision of heaven to forever be more than enough to accomplish the biggest dream He gives you. You won't have to worry about lack. Rick Warren describes it in terms of Jesus paying his taxes: He sends Peter fishing when taxes are due. Peter catches a fish and there is a gold coin in the fish's mouth (Matt.17:27). Rick points out the coins are always going to be there if you are committed to being a "fisher of men."[62]

What if we were to use our abilities, resources and imagination in greater and greater ways to leverage our evangelistic potential? What if our greatest entrepreneurial skills were leveraged in a way that we would be welcomed into heaven by a line of friends, longer than we could have dreamed? What if our greatest concern in life became: "who will be in heaven because of me"? What I know is that our potential to change the world for Jesus would be plenty too much!

I was moved recently to hear the story of Danny Ost, missionary and founder of Faith, Hope and Love Centers in Mexico. After helping plant churches and leading thousands of people to Jesus, he went to heaven in 1985 at a fairly young age. Even in death, he didn't want his mission for Jesus to end. He made plans to be buried in the cemetery outside of Mexico City, where the unclaimed bodies of the poorest of the poor are laid to rest. He purchased space with a pergola-type covering that could hold gospel literature. Since his death, many preachers have held services there.

Today, on the grave marker, there is posted information that shows the telephone numbers of the Faith, Hope and Love Centers in Mexico City.[63] Though he is in heaven, untold numbers of people are still coming to Christ because of his zeal to passionately pursue the lost like Jesus – who left the ninety-nine to rescue the one.

It is this reality that causes us to seek and reach out to people at every opportunity. I believe the words on one gravestone say it best: "Everything I kept, I lost; everything I gave away I still have."

You may have seen the movie *Schindler's List*. Oskar Schindler was a businessman in Germany during the Nazi regime. He was moved to use his resources and influence to buy freedom for hundreds of Jews who were facing certain death in the Holocaust. There is a moving scene near the end of the movie where dozens of survivors come to give thanks and pay tribute to him for his efforts. Rather than being flattered, he breaks down crying. He takes off his watch and screams out, "Ten more! I could've rescued ten more if I had given this." He puts his hands on his car and cries out, "Fifty more. If only I had done more!"[64] What a powerful reminder to all of us who want to impact a world for Christ. What if we would fast-forward our lives to look at our life from heaven's eternal perspective and imagine what our *more* could be while we still have time to achieve it. I believe it is true what C.S. Lewis said, "If you read history, you will find that the Christians who did most for the present world were precisely those who thought most of the next."[65]

Throughout this book, my passionate aim was to stretch you to live every way you can for the bigness of who God wants to be in you and through your life. My prayer is that you will look to the Lord with fresh faith, to stretch and reach to capture the greatest good, blessing, and potential your heart can imagine. And to live a life that expands the dimensions of heaven coming to Earth. I pray that you will long to release as much of the goodness of God as you can, not just for you but for the sake of a broken world. I know you will be so glad you stretched.

May we be certain of this truth articulated by missionary Jim Elliot, who in the prime of his life was martyred trying to reach the Auca Indians of Ecuador for Christ, *"He is no fool who gives what he cannot keep to gain what he cannot lose."*[66]

APPLICATION

Jesus gives us a picture of heaven to keep in our wallet. When we focus on our destination and not our difficulties, the more promising the future looks and the smaller all the problems in our life become.

Try writing everything you are concerned about and put them into two categories: *earth stuff* and *eternity stuff.* Before becoming upset, terrified, preoccupied, or overwhelmed with anything, review which category it's in.

Briefly describe how eternal thinking can change your *today*.

Think eternity: Going through a hard time

Think eternity: Choosing priorities

Think eternity: Family, neighbors, co-workers, community, nations

Think eternity: Jesus is **Plenty too Much***!*

***He is no fool who gives what he cannot keep to gain what he cannot lose.*[67]**

ENDNOTES

Chapter 3: What Is a Plenty too Much Mindset?

1   http://lifespringsresources.com/media/wysiwyg/Renovation_of_ the_Heart_Resource_Guide.pdf, p. 31

2   https://www.goodreads.com/author/quotes/1082290.A_W_ Tozer?auto_login_attempted=true&page=27

Chapter 4: Honey, I shrunk The Lord

3   Beth Moore, Praying God's Word: Breaking Free from Spiritual Strongholds (Nashville: B&H Publishing Group, 2009. p.3)

4   Preaching Today: Sermon Illustrations

5   http://www.wayneandmarthamyers.com

6   Preaching Today: Sermon Illustrations

7   Mark Pfeifer, Breaking a Spirit of Poverty (Morris Publishing; Third Printing Edition, 2007)

Chapter 5: Success Is Who You Are

8   https://www.ziglar.com/product/better-than-good/

9   https://www.myjewishlearning.com/article/jewish-parentchild -relationships/

10 https://faithhopeandpsychology.wordpress.com/2012/03/02/80 -of-thoughts-are-negative-95-are-repetitive/

Chapter 7: Love Is The Key

11 https://www.worldvision.org/hunger-news-stories/blessed -broken-heart

12 https://www.worldvision.org/sponsorship-news-stories/white-jade -first-sponsored-child

13 Daily syndicated newspaper comic strip originally created, written, and illustrated by Hank Ketcham. It debuted on March 12, 1951, in 16 newspapers and was originally distributed by Post-Hall Syndicate.

14   Written by Frederick M. Lehman in 1917, published in Songs That Are Different, Vol. 2 1919. Third stanza was based on the Jewish poem Haddamut, written in Aramaic in 1050 by Meir Ben Isaac Nehorai, a cantor in Worms, Germany.

15   Ibid.

Chapter 8: An Unlikely Partner For A Miracle

16   https://christforthecrescentworld.org/mission-quotes/

Chapter 9: Setting Things In Order/ The Miracle Is In The Management

17   https://www.azquotes.com/quote/571633 and https://www. azquotes.com/quote/528256

18   https://hutchcraft.com/a-word-with-you/your-personal-power/ the-unbaptized-hand-4055

Chapter 10: Discovering Abundance By Putting The Needs And Interests Of Others First

19   https://www.azquotes.com/quote/1465083

20   https://www.brainyquote.com/quotes/james_keller_192856

21   Composers: Roger Cook, Roger Greenaway, Bill Backer, Billy Davis, William Backer

22   https://www.goodreads.com/quotes/63168-i-can-do-things-you-cannot-you-can-do-things

23   https://www.goodreads.com/quotes/50997-the-most-terrible-poverty-is-loneliness-and-the-feeling-of

24   Robert Rector, Marriage: America's Greatest Weapon Against Child Poverty, September 16, 2010, Robert Rector, Senior Research Fellow Robert is a leading authority on poverty, welfare programs and immigration in America.

25   Peanuts by Charles Schulz, January 5,1964

26   https://www.soulshepherding.org/pray-success-competitors/

27   https://www.goodreads.com/quotes/8703-he-drew-a-circle -that-shut-me-out--heretic-rebel

28   https://sermons.faithlife.com/sermons/41544-forgiveness-corrie-meets-guard

Chapter 11: Tapping Into The Abundance Of God Through Prayer

29   Jack Hayford, Prayer Is Invading The Impossible (Alachua: Bridge-Logos,1977).

30   https://biblehub.com/greek/3686.htm (Helps Word-Studies 1987, 2011)

31 https://en.wikipedia.org/wiki/WEC_International

32 Norman Grubb, Touching The Invisible, Chapter 2 (originally published in 1940).

33 A.W. Tozer https://www.goodreads.com/author/quotes/1082290 .A_W_Tozer

34 Henry and Richard Blackaby and Claude King, Experiencing God (B&H Publishing Group, 2009).

Chapter 12: Releasing God's Abundance Through Service Of Ordinary People

35 https://vineyardusa.org/about/history/

36 https://www.youtube.com/watch?v=bY8dhiOc918

37 http://tifwe.org/wp-content/uploads/2013/10/Priesthood-of-All-Believers_Final.pdf

38 http://quozio.com/quote/06b88dc6#!t=1035

39 Wayne Cordeiro, Leading on Empty: Refilling Your Tank and Renewing Your Passion

Chapter 13: An Abundance Mindset For Ministry- Priests And Kings

40 This is a film quote by the Japanese Admiral Isoroku Yamamoto regarding the 1941 attack on Pearl Harbor by forces of Imperial Japan. https://en.wikipedia.org/wiki/Isoroku_Yamamoto%27s_sleeping_giant_quote

41 Source unknown https://christforthecrescentworld.org/mission-quotes/

42 https://www.quotes.net/mquote/16621

43 And I tell you [learn from this], make friends for yourselves [for eternity] by means of the wealth of unrighteousness [that is, use material resources as a way to further the work of God], so that when it runs out, they will welcome you into the eternal dwellings. (Lk 16:9 AMP)

44 http://www.giantsforgod.com/rg-letourneau/

45 https://en.wikipedia.org/wiki/R._G._LeTourneau

46 https://www.letu.edu/about/vision-mission-values.html

47 https://www.britannica.com/biography/George-Washington-Carver

48 https://www.thefreelibrary.com/Man+of+science--and+of+God%3A+George+Washington+Carver+believed+that...-a0112794990

49 https://www.christianquotes.info/quotes-by-author/george-washington-carver-quotes/

50   https://www.goodreads.com/author/quotes/1495762.George_
     Washington_Carver?page=2
51   https://www.thefreelibrary.com/Man+of+science--and+of+God%
     3A+George+Washington+Carver+believed+that...-a0112794990

Chapter 14: Living Out Of The Overflow Of Contentment

52   https://www.azquotes.com/quote/952503
53   https://www.desiringgod.org/books/desiring-god
54   Richard Wurmbrand, Tortured for Christ, first published in Great
     Britain, copyright 1967. Voice of the Martyrs, Inc, Tortured for
     Christ, (Colorado Springs, David C. Cook Publishing), 2018.
55   https://www.goodreads.com/quotes/661017-the-real-measure-of
     -our-wealth-is-how-much-we

Chapter 15: Eternal Perspective-Thinking As Big As Heaven

56   https://www.epm.org/resources/2010/Jan/21/florence-
     chadwick-and-fog/
57   http://cleolampos.com/henry-morrison-and-teddy -roosevelt-
     welcome-home/
58   https://www.goodreads.com/quotes/98267-i-believe
     -like-a-child-that-suffering-will-be-healed
59   https://historyswomen.com/history-in-the-making/
     joni-eareckson-tada/
60   https://www.joniandfriends.org/kneeling/
61   https://sermonquotes.com/authors/9571-i-value-all-things.html
62   http://pastors.com/it-costs-to-reach-your-community-and-its-
     worth-it/
63   https://mrcpartners.org/danny-ost-biography/
64   https://www.quotes.net/mquote/82956
65   https://www.brainyquote.com/quotes/c_s_lewis_151466
66   https://www.brainyquote.com/quotes/jim_elliot_189244
67   Ibid.

CPSIA information can be obtained
at www.ICGtesting.com
Printed in the USA
FSHW021739210520
70347FS

9 781630 505448